FORSYTH LIBRARY - FHSU
344.730326S634i 1983
main   The law and

2 1765 0005 7053 4

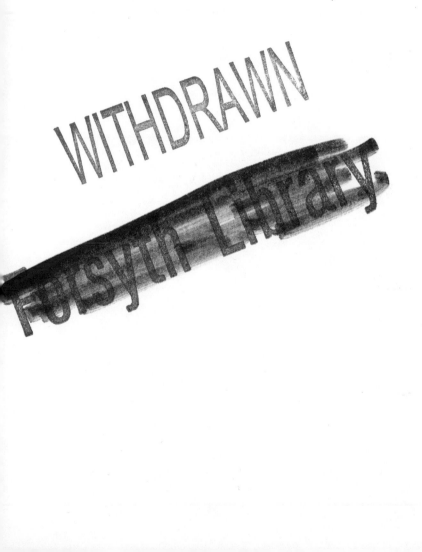

Legal Almanac Series No. 80

THE LAW
AND
LEGISLATION
OF ELDERLY ABUSE

Compiled and edited by
IRVING J. SLOAN

1983
OCEANA PUBLICATIONS, INC.
London • Rome • New York

Library of Congress Cataloging in Publication Data

Sloan, Irving J.
　The law and legislation of elderly abuse.

　(Legal almanac series ; no. 80)
　Includes index.
　1. Aged—United States—States—Abuse of—
Popular works.　I. Title.　II. Series.
KF9324.Z95S56　　1982　　344.73'0326　　82-19045
ISBN 0-379-11143-8　　　　347.304326

© Copyright 1983 Oceana Publications, Inc.

All rights reserved. No part of this publication may be reproduced or transmitted in any form or by any means, electronic or mechanical, including photocopy, recording, xerography, or any information storage and retrieval system, without permission in writing from the publisher.

Manufactured in the United States of America

TABLE OF CONTENTS

INTRODUCTION

The abuse, neglect and exploitation of the
elderly has only recently been recognized as a
problem that requires public policy and intervention. For this reason there is not yet a full
body of legislation let alone case law dealing
with this subject. Nevertheless, the editors of
this Legal Almanac Series concluded that there
should be even at this early stage of the development of the law and legislation of elderly abuse
a volume which brings together presently available material on the subject.

This explains, then, why unlike other titles
in this Series, the present volume is essentially
a work of compilation and editing from the vast
and varied literature on the topic. It is believed
that the readers of the Legal Almanac Series
will welcome a distillation of the information
in a readable, compact format such as the Almanacs
provide.

Most states have some type of protective services program that provides services to persons
eighteen and over who are unable to provide for
their own health, safety and welfare. The Senate
Special Committee on Aging survey in 1980 identified 25 states which have some type of adult
protective services legislation. However, the
provisions and coverage of these laws vary widely
in scope, as do the provisions of the reporting
laws, a subset of the adult protective services
legislation. The summary chart included in this
volume indicates sixteen states with reporting
legislation for adult or elder abuse and protective services. Other states provide the mandate
for a protective services system without reporting provisions. The majority of the sixteen reporting statutes were passed within the last five
years, and similar legislation is now pending in

several additional states. An Oceana Publications loose leaf service, <u>Protection of Abused Victims:</u> <u>State Laws & Decisions</u>, will maintain an update on developments in this field.

Guardianship and civil commitment procedures have been the legal interventions commonly applied in cases of incapacitated or legally incompetent persons. Many states now have domestic violence legislation, directed mainly at spouse abuse, and establishing civil remedies and injunctive relief for victims of domestic violence. In addition, sanctions have been established in the Penal Code regarding abuse or injury to an individual of any age. But these remedies do not specifically address the special problems arising in cases of elder abuse. Such cases typically involve a victim who is unable or unwilling to seek assistance or to initiate civil or criminal proceedings. The victim is frequently in a dependent position and frail, confused or ignorant of the societal protection mechanisms available. Weak enforcement and mechanisms and the difficulty of prosecuting a case of elder maltreatment contribute to the inadequacy of these civil and criminal remedies in addressing the problem of elder abuse.

Basically, the legislation reviewed in this volume requires certain persons to report suspected cases of abuse, neglect or exploitation to a central agency. Mandates for that agency to investigate and arrange voluntary and involuntary service provisions are included to varying degrees in the statutes. Procedures for provision of involuntary service to clients through court intervention also vary widely. The authority vested in the investigating agency, the criteria for emergency intervention and the protection of due process rights are not standardized among the statutes. Definitions of abuse, neglect and exploitation generally encompass the same components in the reporting statutes, although these categories overlap in certain statutes. The lack of uniform definitions, standards and procedures is a common problem of the reporting legislation as a whole. Vague or unclear definitions and stipulations are also common in the legislation.

Due to their recent development, statutes are in an evolutionary stage. Many of the statutes have been amended since passage, as the implementors identify gaps in the design of the laws. Confidentiality provisions, provisions for criminal penalties, and provisions for emergency service to clients, are the topics undergoing the greatest change and development.

This volume is a measured attempt to offer the general reader a broad view of the social, as well as the legislative and legal elements of elderly abuse. Therefore, pieces from a variety of research studies dealing with the nature and the causes of abuse against the elderly are presented in the opening chapters.

However tentative the present state of the law and legislation is on this subject, it is useful to have an organized survey of current information such as this Almanac represents.

Chapter 1
THE NATURE OF ELDER ABUSE:
CASE HISTORIES*

A. PHYSICAL ABUSE

Physical abuse is conduct or violence which results in bodily harm or hurt, excluding mental distress, fright, or emotional disturbance.

- A 92-year-old Massachusetts woman was admitted to a hospital emergency room severely beaten, severely bruised, and with a skull fracture. She died a week later. A son and daughter-in-law, with whom the bed-ridden woman lived, are considered suspects in her death.
- A Massachusetts grandmother's death resulted when her grandson allegedly shot her then apparently burned the house down to cover up the crime. It was only when the medical examiner examined the victim that the gunshot wound was discovered. The case is being prosecuted under a criminal indictment. It was later learned that the grandmother had been physically assaulted by her grandson on several occasions in past years.
- Caseworkers in Ohio investigated reports of mistreatment of an 86-year-old woman who lived with her son. The son protested that he had given his mother "wonderful care, that he fed her daily, brushed her hair and bathed her. The woman was found living in filthy conditions. It was learned that the son had left the victim naked in bed all day and be-

---

*Source: Summary of "Elder Abuse: An Examination of a Hidden Problem," a report by the U.S. House Select Committee on Aging, submitted for the Record by Chairman John L. Burton, Hearing, 97th Congress, First Session, Comm. Pub. No. 97-297, U.S. Govt. Printing Office, Washington: 1981

cause of malnourishment, she had lost considerable weight. She weighed only 80 pounds when discovered by caseworkers. The sister of the victim who alerted authorities was unwilling to press charges. The woman died a month later.

-An elderly District of Columbia person who lived with a daughter-in-law, was often found with bruises on her face and head, ostensibly from falls. The older person was not given medication and was sometimes found dehydrated. She was sent to the hospital where death occurred.

-Another District of Columbia woman 80-years-old was found beaten to death and her acting caregiver was charged with homicide. Detectives said the motive was robbery.

- A complete bed care patient in D.C. was murdered, by the son-in-law, an alcoholic who was left with total care of the patient when his wife was admitted to the hospital with mental problems.

-The North Carolina County Department of Social Services reported finding a 91-year-old widow lying on her bed. She had multiple severe bruises on her face, hands, arms and chest. She was incoherent and confused. She was assessed to have been beaten approximately a week before. The daughter of the elderly woman had been beaten by her own son, also, and that was why she had not reported her own mother's condition. The elderly woman was transported to an emergency room where she eventually died. Her grandson is being held on charged of murder.

A number of State Human Service Departments provided dramatic examples of sexual abuse of their elderly residents:

-A 69-year-old woman from Iowa in day care complained of abdominal pain and vaginal bleeding. She revealed she had been raped by her brother-in-law, with whom she and her husband had lived after being evicted from their home. After reporting the problem, she filed charges against her brother-in-law who was jailed and is awaiting trial.

- Iowa also reported that an arthritic, slightly obese but otherwise healthy woman lived with her daughter and 22-year-old grandson who reportedly physically and sexually abused her. The daughter admitted there was familial conflict and wanted her mother to move. The mother was turning over $300 of her $320 monthly Social Security check to the daughter.
- In the District of Columbia, an 80-year-old woman, a paraplegic, had been sexually abused over a 6-year period by her son-in-law, who beat her with a hammer when she refused his advances.
- New Jersey reported that an hispanic lady of about 74 was assaulted physically and sexually by her son-in-law. The daughter was fully aware of the on-going situation, and warned her mother not to say anything for if she did she would be made homeless. Neighbors and relatives reported the case for protective services.
- In an Ohio nursing home, aide reported that a 96-year-old patient was raped by another aide.

Many of the cases reviewed by the Committee were committed by those with alcohol and drug-related problems:
- An 83-year-old D.C. woman was forced to live with her alcoholic, brain damaged daughter, who neglected and physically and verbally attacked her.
- A bedridden elderly man from the District was brutally beaten by his grandson when he reportedly was under the influence of alcohol.
- An alcoholic caregiver in D.C. beat his elderly client, leaving the patient lying in urine on wrinkled bed linens.
- A 90-year-old bedridden D.C. patient lived with her alcoholic daughter and son-in-law in an unsafe apartment with no door lock. The patient, when found, was covered with bedsores and multiple facial wounds.
- A 78-year-old wealthy D.C. woman was beaten with a phone receiver by her 17-year-old

adopted son. She declined to press charges or to sign a petition for a protective order. The son continues to live with her, receiving a large allowance and driving fancy sport cars. He is suspected of taking drugs.

Apart from discovering that many of the abusers who physically assault older relatives have alcohol problems, the Committee further discovered that many of the abusers suffer from mental disorders. For example:

-Missouri reported that a 71-year-old white woman lived with her 36-year-old son and 39-year-old daughter, both of whom were retarded. There was documentation of several minor physical attacks by the son. The third attack was major and required that the mother be hospitalized because of her critical condition. She remained in the hospital for four weeks and was then transferred to a foster home placement. Her absence from the household led to the eventual institutionalization of these two adult children.

Although the majority of the physical assault cases reviewed by the Committee involve abusive behavior on the part of immediate family members, we found that caregivers were, at times, also responsible for such attacks. For example:

-An elderly New York patient was forced to eat leftovers by her caregiver, was covered with bruises and sores all over her body as a result of repeated beatings by the caregiver, and finally was forced into a hospital.

-An elderly woman in New Hampshire was brought to a hospital emergency room by her caregiver boyfriend. She had a fractured shoulder, had been punched in the face and knocked unconscious, and her upper ribs were black and blue. The house where the patient, caregiver boyfriend and a second male lived was filthy and alcohol bottles were scattered throughout the residence.

-New Jersey reported that an elderly man was assaulted physically by a boarding home operator, receiving injury that resulted in an occluded femoral artery.

-New Jersey also reported the case of a men-

tally retarded elderly client who would be
seen from time to time in church sufficiently
bruised and battered to raise suspicious
questions about the care he was receiving in
a boarding home. It was found that the abuse
was perpetrated by someone in the home.
-A 70-year-old woman from the District of
Columbia was found to be routinely victimized, physically and mentally, by her maid
who would tie her with wire to the bed,
leave her alone for periods of time and deny
her the use of personal items. The older
woman was obviously nervous and unable to
talk in the presence of the maid. At an appropriate time, she revealed that the maid
did tie her to the bed as a punishment for
misbehaving, and that she signed over her
checks to the maid. She had been forced to
turn over to the maid approximately $5000
in the previous few months. The maid also
removed the phone from her room to prevent
her from communicating with the outside
world. The older woman was forced to give the
maid her car and pay towing charges on it.
When she did not comply readily, she would
be pushed from her wheelchair. She was terrified because she had been pushed in such a
manner that twice she suffered a broken hip
and once a broken clavicle. Nursing home
placement was also threatened. Eventually,
the maid was indicted on extortion, false
imprisonment, first degree grand theft and
misrepresenting a licensed nurse.

It is the perceived threat of repeated beatings, denial of daily requirements, and sexual
assaults which occasionaly lead some older
people to fight back in self-defense. Such was
the situation encountered by an elderly father
in the District of Columbia who was charged
with involuntary manslaughter after his son
died during a scuffle with him. The elderly
man said he just couldn't stand the son beating him up anymore.

B. NEGLIGENCE

Negligence can be defined as conduct which is careless; it is the breach of a duty which results in injury to a person or in a violation of rights. There is ample evidence of negligence by relatives and caretakers with devastating consequences to the elderly.

- In South Carolina, a 79-year-old woman who was recuperating from a stroke was kept in an unheated porch attached to her daughter's $90,000 house. The family refused to buy soft foods and to otherwise accept responsibility for the victim who became dehydrated and required hospitalization.
- In the same State, a 68-year-old woman living with her daughter was found by a caseworker in conditions of unspeakable squalor. The woman was kept in an unheated portion of the house where the temperature was measured at less than 20 degrees. When found, the woman had eight soiled blankets piled over her head to keep her warm and the urine from her catheter was frozen. She was also found to be malnourished. She developed pneumonia and was hospitalized. Under discharge, authorities had her placed in a nursing home.
- Washington State reported that they were alerted by concerned neighbors who noticed social security checks delivered monthly and yet they had not seen a woman they knew as "granny" for over a year. Caseworkers arrived at the home where the woman lived with her daughter and grandsons but could not approach the home because of vicious dogs. They returned with the police and representatives of the humane society. The elderly woman was found locked in an upstairs room, dirty, disheveled, incontinent and malnourished. The victim requested that she be relocated to a nursing home.
- An elderly woman in New Jersey living with her daughter and son-in-law was systemmatically neglected. She was left at home all day without food. At night her potty chair

6

and walker were removed so that she could
not get up and go to the bathroom. Her personal correspondence was withheld and her
telephone calls intercepted. One day the
woman fell and was left alone to lie for
about eight hours on the floor with a broken hip. When interviewed, the daughter
said that she wanted her mother dead so that
there would be no more problems. The woman
was olaced in a nursing home by authorities.
-An elderly paraplegic Arkansas woman had been
hospitalized three times for surgery. Her
husband refused to place her in a nursing
home because he wanted continued access to
his wife's Federal Supplementary Security
Income check. The man was an alcoholic and
used the proceeds to support his habit. It
was learned by investigation that during
the day he would load his wife into the
back of his pickup truck and leave her there
while he would go to drink beer at a local
poolhall. During the woman's subsequent
fourth hospital stay, the husband died in
a fire which broke out in the couple's
house trailer. The woman was then placed in
a long-term care facility.
-In Washington, an 84-year-old woman, terminally ill with cancer, was refused proper medical attention by her grandson who
did not want the woman's property and income dissipated by doctor and hospital payments, The woman was found in tremendous
pain, living in truly wretched conditions.
The victim was transferred to a nursing
home where she died a few weeks later.
-Caseworkers in West Virginia were alerted
that an 80-year-old couple might be having
problems. Upon investigation they found the
husband ill to the point of being comatose.
The man was described as "unable to respond,
barely breathing with eyes glazed." The wife
was exhausted and distraught from trying to
care for her husband to the point where her
mental condition was unstable. The wife
would not allow authorities to remove the
man to a hospital for treatment. She charged

7

them with engaging in a plot to take her
husband away from her. Caseworkers contacted the couple's daughter to assist them in
persuading the wife that the man needed
attention. They were unsuccessful and the
husband died two days thereafter.

C. FINANCIAL ABUSE (EXPLOITATION)

Financial abuse or exploitation involves the
theft or conversion of money or anything of value
belonging to the elderly by their relatives or
caretakers. Sometimes, this theft or misappropriation is accomplished by force--sometimes at gun-
point. In other cases, it is accomplished by
stealth through deceit, misrepresentation and
fraud. In most instances, the loss of property by
the elderly is immediate, but in a few instances,
involving undue influence in the writing of wills,
greedy family members have been willing to wait
a few months or even years to acquire the property of a loved one. Examples of financial abuse of
the elderly follow:

-In Arizona, an 88-year-old bedridden, mentally incompetent woman who was being cared
for by a young relative was placed in the
cheapest available boarding home. Her stay
at the home was paid for with the woman's
social security check of $300 a month.
Thereafter, the young relative began to
spend the victim's $20,000 life savings.
When caseworkers investigated, the victim
was found suffering from bedsores and dehydration. In fact, the woman was so dehydrated according to official reports, that
her lips were stuck together. Employees of
the boarding home would not give the woman
fluids because they didn't want her wetting
the bedsheets. After an investigation, the
victim was removed to a nursing home where
she received proper nursing and medical
care.
-In the same State, a woman who had worked
for over 30 years and who enjoyed a liberal
pension, suffered two broken hips at the age

8

of 88. An acquaintance arranged for her to
be placed in an unlicensed boarding home.
Within two weeks, the owners had either
forged the victim's name to checks or had
her forced to sign over $2,300 in checks to
them. The investigation revealed that the
woman was purposely overmedicated in order
to keep her in a stupor. The woman had numerous stocks and bonds which apparently had
been misappropriated. Social workers hired
an attorney to institute legal proceedings
to recover funds inappropriately taken and
moved the victim to a licensed nursing home
where she is reportedly receiving excellent
care.
-Also in Arizona, an 84-year-old World War I
veteran with a diagnosis of congestive heart
failure came under the influence of a "friend"
who obtained the old man's power of attorney
and opened joint bank accounts with him. The
"friend" represented that the man had no
relatives. Investigators learned of the case
when the man was brought to the emergency
room of a local hospital. The old man was
malnourished, dehydrated and maggots had infested under his skin. Investigators learned
that approximately $20,000 had been taken.
Relatives were located in Florida and Michigan but they refused to accept responsibility for the man so a guardian was appointed
by the court to revoke the power of attorney
and recover the man's assets. Both the old
man and State social workers were physically
threatened but ultimately they were successful in recovering an automobile and much of
the other financial assets. The man was
placed in a county nursing home.
-California officials report that an 87-year-
old widow in frail health and generally confined to a wheelchair, unable to care for
her day-to-day needs, was allegedly the
victim of physical and financial abuse from
1974 through 1980. A nurse companion who was
also her conservator and three children depleted her financial resources by more than
$300,000 while depriving the woman of prop-

er medical attention, food or clothing. Caseworkers helped the woman to institute legal
proceedings.
- In Atlanta a man in his sixties and his wife
were financially abused by their 23-year-old
son who stole from them and broke into their
house when locked out after he had refused
to work or leave the home. When the police
refused to arrest him on three different
occasions, and the warrant officer said he
could not help the family, the father shot
the son in the leg the next two times he
broke in.
- A 77-year-old woman in Atlanta was abused
verbally by her 23-year-old grandson whom
she was supporting from a small fixed income. On occasions he would steal her money.

D. PSYCHOLOGICAL ABUSE (EMOTIONAL)

In addition to being abused physically and
financially, the elderly can also suffer emotional or psychological abuse at the hands of their
relatives. At one end of the spectrum, psychological abuse includes simple name calling and
verbal assaults. At the other end, it is a protracted and systematic effort to dehumanize the
elderly, sometimes with the goal of driving a
person to insanity or suicide. There are few
things more pernicious in life than the constant
threat by caretakers to throw the elderly into
the street or have them committed to mental institutions. The most common weapon used in this
warfare is the threat of nursing home placement.
By its nature, psychological abuse usually exists
in combination with one or more other abuses.
Following are some examples:

- In Massachusetts, a daughter-in-law harbored
great resentment of her mother-in-law for
whose care she was responsible. The daughter-
in-law refused to contribute to the woman's
support. The daughter-in-law converted her
mother's-in-law social security check to her
own use--often to buy alcohol. Over a long
period of time, the elderly woman was ver-

bally abused, threatened, and in fact, the daughter-in-law did periodically beat the woman. When this matter came to the attention of the police, they discovered that the daughter-in-law put the woman's food on the floor, telling her she was an animal and that she would be required to eat like one.

-A report from Delaware tells of a daughter-in-law who would keep her husband's widowed mother confined to the basement without social contacts. Anytime the widow tried to leave this captivity, she was verbally assaulted. After the widow broke her arm in a fall, the daughter-in-law added physical force, severely twisting the woman's broken arm on several occasions.

-An 87-year-old woman in Massachusetts was psychologically abused by her middle-aged son. On a visit to her on a day when she was not feeling well, he proceeded to discuss what monies she had, what insurance and what brothers or sisters of his were to get her property in the event of her death. The conversation disturbed her greatly and the day after the discussion she went to bed, and never got out of it. One month later, she was dead.

-In California, an 87-year-old woman in ill-health, confined to a wheelchair, and unable to care for her daily needs, was repeatedly and systematically abused by her family and nurse companions. The mental and physical torture lasted six years. During this time, the woman was threatened, held prisoner, deprived of all contact with the outside world, not permitted to see friends and family, and battered.

TABLE 1*

CHARACTERISTICS OF ABUSED ELDERS

Category		%	Category		%
Age:	Mean	84	Race:	White	88%
	Range	60-92		Black	12%
Religion:	Protestant	61%	Sex:	Female	81%
	Catholic	8%		Male	19%
	Jewish	4%	Degree of Physical Impairment:	Bedridden	19%
	Unknown	27%		Impaired Mobility	19%
Economic Status:	Retired, on pension	27%		Can't prepare food	62%
	Lower Class	15%		Can't take own medication	54%
	Middle Class	58%		Needs help to keep clean	62%
	Upper Class	0%		None	4%
Living Arrangements, live with	Children	46%	Degree of Mental Impairment:	Severe	12%
	Spouse	23%		Moderate	35%
	Grandchildren	31%		Mild	15%
	Other Relatives	8%		None	15%
	Unrelated Caretaker	12%		No response	23%
	Nursing Home	8%			
	Alone	4%			

*Source: M.R. Block & J.D. Sinnott, The Battered Elder Syndrome: An Exploratory Study, Center on Aging, University of Maryland, College Park (1979)

12

TABLE 2

CHARACTERISTICS OF ABUSERS

Age:			Economic Status:		
	Teens	12%		Lower Class	12%
	Young Adults (20s-30s)	8%		Middle Class	65%
	Middle-Aged (40s-50s)	53%		Upper Class	4%
	Young-Old (60s-70s)	8%	**Relation to Victim:**		
	Old-Old (80+)	11%		Children (includes in-laws)	42%
	Unknown	8%		Spouse	15%
Race:				Grandchildren	19%
	White	88%		Other Relatives	4%
	Black	12%		Unrelated Caretakers	19%
Sex:			**Reason for Abuse:**		
	Female	58%		Psychological	58%
	Male	42%		Economic	31%
Religion:				Unknown	11%
	Protestant	35%	**Prior Abuse Incidents:**		
	Catholic	8%		Yes	58%
	Jewish	4%		No	4%
	Unknown	53%		Unknown	38%

TABLE 3

FREQUENCY OF TYPES OF ABUSE*

Physical Abuse Sustained:

none apparent	15%
bruises, welts	31%
sprains, dislocations	4%
malnutrition	4%
freezing	4%
abrasions, lacerations	8%
wounds, cuts, punctures	4%
bone fractures	8%
skull fractures	4%
direct beatings	15%
lack of personal care	38%
lack of food	19%
lack of supervision	38%
tied to bed	8%
tied to chair	4%

Psychological Abuse Sustained:

verbal assault	58%
threat	46%
fear	50%
isolation	58%

Material Abuse Sustained:

theft of money or property	12%
misuse of money or property	46%

Rating of Environment:

dirt in house	38%
vermin in house	8%
inadequate heat	4%
smell like urine	19%
no food in house	8%

*categories are not mutually exclusive

14

Chapter 2
CAUSES OF ELDER ABUSE*

As is the case with most social problems, it is difficult to determine the specific cause or causes of elder abuse, particularly with the limited knowledge base that now exists. Most experts do appear to believe, however, that a major precipitating factor is family stress. Meeting the daily needs of a frail, dependent elderly relative may be an intolerable burden for family members. The resulting frustration may sometimes be expressed in violent behavior.

Americans live in a violent society. In Behind Closed Doors, a recently published book on family violence, it was noted that the first national study of violence in American homes estimated that every other house in America is the scene of family violence at least once a year. Author Richard Gelles states:

> We have always known that America is a violent society. A war in Vietnam, a riot in Watts, a gangland slaying, a political assassination or a rape in an alley are all types of violence familiar to Americans. What is new and surprising is that the American family and the American home are perhaps as or more violent than any other single American institution or setting (with the exception of the military, and only then in time of war). Americans run

---

*Source: U.S. House Select Committee on Aging, Hearing, 97th Congress, First Session, Comm. Pub. No. 97-297, U.S. Govt. Printing Office, Washington: 1981, pp.195-199.

the greatest risk of assault, physical
injury, and even murder in their own
homes by members of their own families.

That family violence occurs, in whatever
form- child battering, wife beating, or elder
abuse- is so shocking and repulsive that many
are reluctant to believe it or understand what
brings such behavior to pass. No one theory provides the entire explanation for the cause of
family violence. Experts generally agree, however, that any one or a combination of any of the
following factors may explain why our elders are
abused by their loved ones.

A. RETALIATION

Some experts surmise that elder abuse is a
form of retaliation, or revenge, in which the
abuser was mistreated as a child and returns to
abuse the parent. For example, in a University
of Michigan study at the Institute of Gerontology,
investigators hypothesized that abusers are often
the "battered child grown old." Mistreated as
children, they become abusive parents themselves,
both of their children, and later on, of their
older parent.

In some cases, the elderly are reaping what
they sowed. According to a study conducted by Dr.
Suzanne Steinmetz, University of Delaware professor, children treated non-violently as they
grow up attack their parents later on by 1 in
400; however, if a child is mistreated violently
by the parent, the chance they'll attack their
parents later on is 1 in 2.

Chicago psychiatrist Mitchell Messer, whose
clients include adults caring for elderly parents,
stated: "We find parent beatings when the parents
set the example of solving problems through bru-
tality when the children were growing up. If an
elderly parent continues to bait their vulnerable
child, the response is simply following the example his parents set."

There are often unresolved conflicts and re-
sentments existing between the generations. Some
adult children appear almost castrated emotionally
from a history of parent abuse. Their reaction is
to strike back. This may be compounded if the
elderly parent continues to bait their vulnerable
child. The response is violent aggression. Former
social worker, Agnes McRoberts of Houston, in an
article in **Dynamic Years**, states that battered
parent cases she has seen follow a typical pattern, involving a "symbiotic relationship" in
which an alcoholic daughter or son and an aging
mother are mutually dependent on one another.
The mother is indulgent, compulsive and clinging.
She suddenly cuts off money to her adult child
which triggers anger, resentment and abuse, particularly when the adult child has been drinking.

B. <u>VIOLENCE AS A WAY OF LIFE</u>

Another rationale for elder abuse is thought
by some to be the widespread acceptance of violence in American society, which fosters a cli-
mate in which it is acceptable to express frustration and stress in violent ways. In some
families, patterns of violence exist from generation to generation, as a normal response to
stress. In a study of Intergenerational Family
Violence, Dr. Elizabeth Rathbone-McCuan of Washington University in St. Louis sees the family
as an excellent breeding ground of violence and
a social unit subject to interpersonal stresses,
internal and external strains and experiences
which create conflict among family members. She
reported, "Since violence can and does occur
within the family setting, and since the society
in general holds predominantly negative attitudes
toward the aged person, the likelihood of physical
attack or other abuses of the aged person by the
family members is worthy of additional consideration."

Researchers in a Cleveland-based study also
believe there are family patterns of violence
which continue from generation to generation:

"Violence is the normative response to stress in some families, and patterns of long-term family conflict, bickering and intentional generation of negative responses can pre-exist the current abuse by many years." Also, unresolved conflict, from childhood or mid-life, can cause an elderly relative to become a burden carried with great stress and ambivalence which increases the risk of abuse.

C. LACK OF CLOSE FAMILY TIES

In some families where there is little or no closeness of a relationship between the adult children and their parents, a sudden appearance of a dependent elderly parent can precipitate stress and frustration without the love and friendship necessary to counteract the new responsibilities of the adult children. For a large part of their lives, many elderly are not able to integrate themselves with the lives of their children. Sometimes, this is due to geographical distance or sometimes emotional distance. Thus, when such an elderly person is unable to live independently they may reunite with their children after many years of separation. The elderly parent can become resented as an intruder, and abuse follows. For example, a counselor reported that a son was determined he and his wife would care for his elderly father. However, the burden of the care fell on the wife who had never gotten along with her father-in-law. She felt the pressure of caring for the older man, the pressure of caring for her own family. She began to beat the father-in-law. He was finally removed from the home, after counselors convinced the family it had to be done.

D. LACK OF FINANCIAL RESOURCES

"Under such circumstances as lack of money and the stress of dealing with a dependent older person, normal people often lash out against their elders," states Dr. Steinmetz of the University of Delaware. The pressure and frustrations of family and financial problems is often cited by experts as a factor which drives family members to abusive behavior.

Many families caring for elderly parents or grandparents live on either fixed incomes or strict budgets during these times of increasing inflation, rising unemployment and skyrocketing fuel costs. Also, the increasing medical costs associated with the care of an older family member can often go beyond the depleted savings of the elderly parent and the penny-pinched resources of their children. The stresses associated with insufficient income combined with the inherent stress of providing daily care for an individual who requires a considerable amount of assistance with daily living tasks, can often become overwhelming and precipitate physical abuse and neglect.

Adding to an already tense financial situation is the factor that women, the primary caregivers in families, are increasingly entering the work force. Should this daughter or daughter-in-law quit her job and stay home to care for her elderly parent, thus losing her sense of freedom, independence, as well as financial reward, or should she stay at home to care full-time for the dependent parent? The dilemma is that she will be financially strapped either way. If she works, she must find someone else to care for the parent during the day, and if she does not work she loses the additional income needed by the family, for basic necessities as well as the increased medical bills for the care of the elderly parent.

Unfortunately, this overtaxing of a family's resources is sometimes exacerbated by Federal and State government policies that limit or reduce benefits and services to elderly people when they live with their families. For example, the Federal Supplementary Security Income (SSI) program provides a minimum income floor to low-income aged, blind and disabled individuals. However, when an eligible individual is living in the household of another individual and re-

21

ceiving support or in-kind maintenance from that person, the monthly SSI benefit is reduced by one-third. Another example is the Medicare program, the Federal health insurance program for persons over the age of 65. The Medicare program provides home health services, but they are contingent on numerous requirements and do not cover the on-going non-medical care and services that a dependent elderly person often needs to assist him or her to remain at home.

On the other hand, the Medicaid program, a Federal-State matching program that provides medical assistance for certain low-income persons, including the elderly, is structured to extensively subsidize nursing home care but offers less assistance to elderly individuals who wish to remain in their own home.

Services such as homemaker and chore services, adult day care, and adult protective services are provided by the State under the social services program authorized by Title XX of the Social Security Act. This title provides federally matched funds to the States for wide variety of social services, including many services for the elderly. Eligibility for those programs, excluding adult protective services is limited to SSI and Aid to Families with Dependent Children (AFDC) recipients and individuals and families who have incomes less than 115% of the State's median income, adjusted to family size. This criterion alone excludes many families who, despite their ineligibility, may not be able to afford these services on their own.

Many experts believe that it is this inability to obtain needed services coupled with the lack of financial resources which can build resentment and foster abusive conduct even in the most loving family.

E. RESENTMENT OF DEPENDENCY

Caring for a frail elderly parent, who requires a considerable amount of assistance can be a very draining experience. Oftentimes, the caretaker can become overwhelmed with the infringement this places on his/her own time. A child can feel trapped by the burden of caregiving at a time of anticipated independence from child-rearing. This can lead to frustration, anger and resentment, precipitating some form of abuse.

Many middle-aged family members feel resentment with the sudden intrusion of dependent parents. An example cited in a University of Michigan study is a common one:

> ... a family situation in which the grandparents either gradually or quite suddenly become dependent on their own middle-aged children who are simultaneously experiencing the dependencies of their own teenage or young adult children...similarly, middle-aged adults who have just emerged from the parental role with a new sense of freedom and independence, may also find themselves burdened by the dependencies of their own parents.

The resentment of having to care for their frail, bedridden, often incontinent parent, which ties them to the home pushes many to the breaking point. Often these adult children want to do the right thing, but are unable to cope with the financial and emotional stress required to do so.

Even more frustrating for the adult child can be the hopelessness and despair experienced by their elderly parent as they become more and more dependent and vulnerable. The elderly parent may begin to feel a loss of control over the basic tasks of daily living. This feeling of helplessness can result in a demanding or totally withdrawn patient. Either behavior can be intolerable for the caregiver and lead to frustration and abuse.

A number of letters which came to the House Committee on Aging expressed the resentment which can result from caring for a dependent relative:

We made many sacrifices for my
mother- not being able to go away for
week-ends and vacations when we wanted
to because she could not be left alone.
Fetching and running for her- taking
her where she had to go, fixing the
house for her- the list is endless. And
all the while she occupied an apartment
which was worth hundreds of dollars,
for free. In the end, her lawyer gets
everything-and we were abused by her
because the lies she told everyone about
us were believed by many.

Here, the number of our elderly population exceeds the national average,
I believe; and thus, there are many
aged parents and relatives being cared
for by their families, presumably un-
counted in any survey on the subject.
When this confining situation calls for
one person to put his or her own life
"on hold" because it is necessary to
spend all day and every day as the sole
companion of a demented senile patient,
the unrelieved tension is bound to take
its toll on even the most loving and
gentle custodian.

I think you should explore the child's
side of taking care of the aging parent.
The child, sometimes in their 50's or
60's also has medical problems and di-
minishing strength to cope with the care
of aging parents on a 24-hour basis...
I had to cope with increasing medical
problems of my mother for seven years,
plus my inability to work and lack of
any personal life because of these de-
mands. I experienced this over a year
ago and I still feel emotionally and
physically drained. While giving the
care, I often pushed myself beyond my
limits and this affected my personality
and influenced my ability to give the
type of care I would have liked.

A report, Future Directions for Aging Policy,
A Human Service Model, issued by the Committee of
Aging in 1980, revealed that as many as one out
of every ten dependent older persons will be abused
by their caregiver each year.

F. INCREASED LIFE EXPECTANCY

Associated with dependency is the dramatic
increase in life expectancy, with more people
reaching age 75 and over than ever before in
history. At the same time, the fertility rate
has dropped considerably. This means the dependency period of old age has been extended, leaving caretakers to provide extensive home care for
a longer length of time. It also means there will
be fewer middle-aged adult children to care for
their elderly parents and grandparents. An
Institute of Gerontology study at the University
of Michigan stated:

> It may be that the increasing presence
> of the elderly and their rolelessness is
> a likely contributor to their own vulner-
> ability. It is now likely that in old
> age, people will be dependent upon their
> own children or grandchildren longer than
> their children were dependent upon them.

G. LACK OF COMMUNITY RESOURCES

According to Maggie Kuhn, convenor of the
Gray Panthers- an organization designed to
bridge the gap between young and old populations-
even the best of parent-child relationships can
deteriorate as the burden of care persists over
a long period of time, as noted earlier. Those
children who are financially equipped to maintain their dependent relatives in their homes
oftentimes are unable to find the services in
their communities to assist them to do so. Numerous witnesses have testified before the House
Committee on Aging that few support systems currently exist in local communities for caregivers
to draw upon and those that do exist are virtu-

ally unknown to the average citizen.

Work responsibility, lack of training and
sensitivity, renders the average child helpless
to meet his older relative's specific dietary
and physical requirements. Many children can become overwhelmed by the emotional and financial
responsibility and are simply unable to find the
social and health-in-house home services they
need. Some experts see battering of the elderly
as a natural consequence of inadequate services
to families caring for a frail elderly relative.

H. STRESS AND OTHER LIFE CAUSES

The dramatic change that can occur when a
frail elderly parent moves in with a family
already struggling in several areas of family
relationships produces intense stress. For some
elderly people, constant nursing supervision is
necessary. The care of a dependent person can be
physically and emotionally exhausting and a caregiver can deal with only a certain amount of
stress before reaching the breaking point.
According to Dr. Steinmetz, "the bottom line is
that if you increase the stress on family members
without adding supports to help them cope with
it, you increase the likelihood of violence because a person and a family can handle only so
much."

Most experts tend to agree with Dr. Steinmetz that family stress is a major precipitating
factor in elder abuse. One study found that the
elderly person was a significant source of stress
to the family in 63 percent of the reported abuse
cases.

1. History of Personal or Mental Problems.-
In families where the adult child has a history
of personal or pathological problems, a potential
for abuse exists. In numerous cases reviewed by
the House Committee on Aging, mentally impaired
children were responsible for abusing their
parents. Family members appear to become the
objects of such abusive behavior because of their

26

proximity to the abuser. Some crises triggers the abuser, who strikes out at the nearest person or object.

2. <u>Unemployment</u>.- Unemployment is a major stress-producing experience for most individuals. It is even more stress-producing if unemployment occurs at middle age. Dr. Steinmetz reports that intra-family violence occurs much more frequently when the major income-producing member (generally the male-adult-husband) is unemployed. This theory has proven to be true in many cases of spouse and child abuse and appears to be a significant problem triggering elder abuse.

3. <u>History of Alcohol and Drug Abuse</u>.- The Committee found many instances of abuse wherein the abuser was experiencing alcohol and drug consumption problems. Consistent consumption of alcohol and drugs are readily identifiable as contributing to family violence. Because alcohol acts as a depressant, the effect seems to depress aggression inhibition systems, thus making aggressive behavior much more likely. The following is one such case reported to the Committee in which alcohol appeared to be a precipitating factor:

> A young woman and her husband separate and get a divorce. The couple was living with the husband's mother and one child of their own. When the couple separated, the husband left home while the wife and child stayed with the mother-in-law. She would beat her, cash her social security checks, and feed her like an animal. The daughter-in-law used alcohol frequently.

I. <u>ENVIRONMENTAL CONDITIONS</u>

Certain environmental factors can precipitate stress which may then lead to neglectful or abusive behavior of family members, especially the frail elderly persons forced to seek assistance in the basic tasks of daily living. Quality of housing, unemployment, intra-family conflict, alcohol and drug abuse, neighborhood and crowded living conditions can by themselves or in combination with other factors encourage mistreatment of a dependent elderly person.

Such an example is found in a case study in Lee, New Hampshire in 1978 where a combination of environmental factors precipitated abuse: A 48-year-old son was found guilty of manslaughter, by beating, in the death of his 78-year-old mother. The son lived with his mother in a trailer. The mother was incontinent, unstable on her feet, and required extensive personal care. Health, living conditions and the quality of the mother-son relationship all contributed to the son's frustration, anger and finally physical violence.

> When I was a laddie
> I lived with my granny
> And many a hiding ma granny di'ed me.
> Now I am a man
> And I live with my granny
> And do to ma granny
> What she did to me.

> (traditional rhyme, anonymous)

Chapter 3
SURVEY OF ADULT PROTECTIVE
SERVICES LEGISLATION*

A number of states have adopted legislation,
including abuse reporting laws and protective
services laws, as distinct from guardianship proceedings in an attempt to provide procedures and
remedies for incapacitated adults who are abused,
neglected and exploited. This legislation provides
the mandate to allow for access by social service
workers to investigate for abuse, neglect or exploitation, to require reporting of abuse, neglect
or exploitation with immunity and confidentiality
assured, to affix penalties for violations, and
to allow for voluntary and involuntary provisions
of protective services while safeguarding individual rights against inappropriate intervention.

Eleven states carry some form of an abuse reporting law and protective services law:

> Virginia, Va. Code ¶55.1-55.8; Nebraska,
> Neb. Laws ¶28-1501 et seq; Arkansas,
> Ark. Stat. 1947 Annot. ¶59-1301 et seq;
> Alabama, Ala. Code ¶38-9-1 to 11; North
> Carolina, N.C. Gen. Stat. Art. 4A, ¶108-
> 102 et seq; Florida, Fl. Stat. Ch. 77-
> 336, ¶409.3631 et seq; South Carolina,
> 43 S.C. Laws 29-10 et seq; Connecticut,
> Conn. Gen. Stat. Annot. ¶14 et seq;
> Oklahoma, 43 Okla. Stat. Annot. ¶801-810;
> Kentucky, Ky. Rev. Stat. Ch. 209, 010
> et seq; Tennessee, Tenn. Code Annot.
> ¶14-2301 et seq.

Four states have adopted statutes which provide the mandate for protective services systems
without reporting access or involuntary service

---

*Source: K.J. Meyers & J.A. Bergman, An Analysis
of Elder Abuse Laws in Massachusetts and Other
States, Legal Research & Services for the Elderly,
Boston (1979).

provisions:

> Maine, Maine Rev. Stat. Annot. ¶3601
> et seq; Montana, Mont. Rev. Code 71-
> 1914 et seq; Michigan, Mich. Code Annot.
> 400.14; New Hampshire, N.H. Rev. Stat.
> Ch. 161-D:1 et seq.

An additional two states have protective service
legislation which includes involuntary service provisions but no mandatory reporting and investigating provision:

> Wisconsin, 55 Wis. Stat. Annot. ¶55.00
> 1 et seq; Maryland, Md. Code Annot. Art.
> 88A, ¶106 et seq.

PERSONS COVERED

The premise of the protective services legislation is that persons exist in society who are
unable to care for and/or protect themselves.
Society, in the form of the state, as parens patriae,
assumes the responsibility of this care and protection. The criteria for state intervention is
linked to the existence of abuse, neglect, exploitation and/or abandonment and a functional,
mental, or physical, inability to care for or
protect oneself. The scope of the law and the
determination of need on the part of the persons
covered are defined according to this premise to
assure that vulnerable persons who are abuse
victims are protected and reached by services.

Of the nineteen states with legislation, a
majority of the laws apply to persons "in need
of protective services" or those "incapacitated"
and abused, neglected or exploited. Whereas the
latter is linked to a functional determination,
the former criteria, unless clearly defined in
the legislation, fails to define an actual standard to be applied. In those cases, there is the
possibility of confusion in mandatory reporting
and the increase in the likeliness of inappropriate
intervention. Other legislation relies upon the
medical model of developmentally disabled, in-

firmities of age, and senility, in the determination of the coverage of the law. These states are North Carolina, Florida and South Carolina. These standards, as applied to the elderly, mean the diagnosis of acute or chronic brain syndrome, a condition typically thought to be an organic dysfunction. However, evidence indicates that such a catch-all diagnosis may in fact be a self-fulling prophecy, which masks, at the outset, conditions such as vitamin deficiency, depression, dehydration, over-medication, or other injuries. The failure to treat these conditions because of the original diagnosis results in further deterioration until organic dysfunction actually exists. The physician will often rely on information of the elderly person's condition provided by a caretaker. The opportunity for bias always looms.

A standard linked to functional ability to care and/or protect him/herself and the existence of abuse, neglect, exploitation and abandonment (Connecticut is the only state that presently includes abandonment) defines the class in the manner most likely to include the largest of persons in need, without increasing the likelihood of inappropriate intervention.

Following this logic, all but one state, Virginia, clearly define the determination of need for services to be a question of behavioral or functional capacity. The minority view states that the individual in need lacks sufficient understanding or capacity to make, or communicate responsible decisions. It should be noted that this standard fails to address the central issue of the individual's ability to provide for his or her basic needs. It also bases the determination on the cognitive ability to make "responsible" decisions. This vague and value laden standard opens the door for inappropriate intervention in cases where some surrogate authority decides that a particular decision is not "responsible" irrespective of the individual's ability to function and provide for his/her own needs.

REPORTING AND INVESTIGATION

Eleven states have explicit reporting provisions. Six of these states make reporting mandatory for anyone who has reasonable cause to suspect or believe that an individual is a victim of abuse, neglect, or exploitation. The remaining states restrict reports to either practitioners of the healing arts solely or to a broad category of professionals including physicians, nurses, social workers, etc.

None of the jurisdictions covers the question of confidentiality as it applies to medical practitioners, or clergy persons. The assumption is that the law requires reporting even where confidentiality will be betrayed. This is in keeping with the proposition that the importance or the societal interest in the preservation of these lives is paramount.

Several reporting provisions include a sanction of jail or a fine for failure to report.

Following the filing of a report to the designated agency, that agency is required to investigate and evaluate the circumstances and to make a determination of need. All state laws require either prompt investigation or investigation within a specified period such as 72 hours. This investigation includes, at least, a home visit and consultation with persons knowledgeable about the facts of the case. The ability of the agency to respond to reports is a key issue which is linked to fiscal considerations. Some statutes include provisions limiting agency responsibility depending on availability of funding.

If an investigation indicates that the elderly person is or has been abused, neglected or exploited and is incapacitated or in need of protective services, the agency will either develop a service plan or refer and contract out to another agency to develop such a plan. Voluntary services provision can commence at that point if the individual consents.

These statutory provisions are coupled with
procedures to enable the investigator or service
provider to gain access in cases where access is
denied by a caretaker. In either situation, the
department can petition the court for injunctive
relief to gain access to investigate upon proof
of "reasonable cause to suspect" or to enjoin the
caretaker from interfering in the provision of
services. In the latter case, the petitioner must
allege specific facts or prove by clear, cogent
and convincing evidence (North Carolina) that
protective services are needed, that the individual in question consents to services and that
the caretaker has interfered to prevent service
provision. The purpose of the law here is to make
certain that sufficient evidence is presented
prior to a court order to prevent inappropriate
or nonconsensual intervention.

If services are refused or consent is withdrawn, the case must be closed except where the
department/agency thinks that the individual lacks
the capacity to consent.

INVOLUNTARY SERVICE PROVISION

In some cases, upon investigation the department will find an elderly person who, because of
imminent danger or medical emergency, is in need
of immediate assistance. If consent is secured,
no legal action is needed. If consent is refused.
the department must make an initial determination
of the individual's mental capacity to consent
as well as determining whether an emergency exists. If there is doubt about the elderly person's capacity to consent, involuntary services
may be provided only with court authorization
secured pursuant to the state's guardianship
statute or protective services provisions.

This area of emergency intervention raises
the conflict between state interests and individual rights. There is often a conflict between
the humane impulse to provide services and the

individual's right to refuse services or even access. This conflict raises questions such as, does a person have a right to remain in a dangerous environment if he/she wishes? Must he/she be left exploited or neglected, even to the point of starvation, if he/she chooses?

Basic to our legal system are the individual's right of self-determination and right to privacy. These constitutional rights are an expression of the sanctity of individual free choice as a fundamental constituent of life. But the individual's civil rights are not absolute or without limit. The state (and its agencies) can and does intervene, regulate, and prohibit. State intervention occurs pursuant to two legal doctrines: (1) Police power, which gives the state authority to regulate activities that involve the health and safety of society. (2) Parens patriae, which gives the state authority to act in a parental capacity for persons who cannot care for themselves or who are dangerous to themselves.

Intervention by the state is regulated by balancing the state's interests (under the police power or parens patriae doctrines) against the interests of the individual to be left alone. In child abuse reporting statutes, the states can intervene in the life of a family because it has an overriding interest in the health and welfare of the child.

The parameters of state intervention are often unclear, reflecting historical and social trends. When the state does have the right to intervene in individual lives (under health regulations, social welfare laws, etc.), that right is defined specifically by statute and regulations. The state does not have the right to intervene in a person's life without either the person's consent or statutory authority.

The competent person, however, has the right to refuse social and medical services. The Massachusetts Supreme Court held in Lane v. Candura (1978) that, if an elderly woman was com-

34

TABLE 4

SEVERITY OF ABUSE

	Physical Abuse	Psychological Abuse	Economic Abuse
Mild	17.65%	4.76%	8.33%
Mild-Moderate	5.88%	4.76%	16.67%
Moderate	47.06%	34.92%	33.33%
Moderate-Severe	9.80%	12.70%	25.00%
Severe	19.61%	42.86%	16.67%
Total	100.00%	100.00%	100.00%

petent, she could make her own decision concerning the refusal of "needed" medical treatment, whether or not that decision might seem irrational to others. The court found that Mrs. Candura was competent. The evidence showed that she tended to be stubborn, that she was lucid on some matters and confused on others, that her train of thought wandered, that her conception of time was distorted, that she was sometimes hostile, occasionally defensive, and sometimes combative to questioning, but that she had a high degree of awareness and acuity. The court said that irrational did not mean incompetent.

But the right to refuse services can be limited if the individual is found to be legally incompetent. Under most state laws, limitations on the individual's right to self-determination require the state to present sufficient evidence to meet the statutory criteria for appointment of a guardian or for civil commitment to a mental health facility. Such determinations are only allowable with full due process protections, including the right to counsel.

In a judicial determination of the individual's competence, the court relies on evidence, testimony, the persuasiveness of argument by the attorneys, and other, often intangible, factors such as the inability to think or act for oneself as to personal health, safety, and general welfare, or to make informed decisions as to property, finances, etc.

While state guardianship statutory standards may be similar (many states use the Uniform Probate Code), case law interpreting the standards varies from state to state, and in some instances from community to community. It is in any event clear that the "competent" individual can make an irrational decision to remain in an abusive environment.

Some states, such as Kentucky and Connecticut, do not provide for emergency intervention within the adult protective services statute. These states limit the provision primarily to reporting, and to voluntary service provision with injunctive relief if access has been denied. In these jurisdictions involuntary services may be provided pursuant to established guardianship and commitment procedures. Whereas, in many of these cases, limited intervention would suffice to provide the needed services and support to the infirm elderly, forced reliance or guardianship or commitment most likely will result in the imposition of more drastic and extensive limitations, contrary to the notion of the least restrictive alternative. Or, the agency staff are encouraged to use deception or coercion to influence the victim to accept services, regardless of the individual's physical or mental status. Further, if the state does not have provisions for a public guardian, this option is usually not available for persons not financially able.

Statutes in states such as Alabama and Florida are even more extreme in this regard. The Alabama statutes states "If the person is incapable of giving consent or does not consent, the department shall petition the court for an order authorizing the department to arrange for care for such person immediately. Upon a determination by the court that such care is urgently and immediately necessary... an appropriate order... shall be issued ... to arrange for the placement of such person in an approved foster home, licensed nursing home, or other similar facility immediately (Ala. Code ¶38-9-5). Notice of a hearing on the merits of protective placement must be given within ten days and, if read in conjunction with the provisions on protective placement, a hearing must be held within 30 days of filing of such petition. This statute does not include emergency service provision, but focuses solely on involuntary protective placement for persons unable and unwilling to consent. There is no question of competency here. Thus, the individual who is competent and refuses services, may still be the subject of involuntary protective placement.

According to Florida's Adult Protective Services Act (Fla. Stat. Ch.77-336, ¶409.3631), involuntary removal and placement can take place when authorized by court order. Although a preliminary hearing must be held within forty-five hours to establish probable cause for protective placement, custody can be continued for four days pending a hearing on the need for continuing services. These provisions do not include the right of representation, the individual's right to be present or notice requirements. The statute does not provide for a determination of the individual's lack of capacity to consent, also prerequisite to involuntary placement. The only criteria spelled out in the statute is that an individual suffering from the infirmities of aging who is being abused, maltreated or neglected, may be subject to this procedure. These standards may be insufficient when held up against the constitutional guarantees of due process. Arkansas and South Carolina have similar possible inadequacies.

Other states, such as Tennessee, Virginia, North Carolina, Oklahoma, and Maryland, provide in varying degree, due process safeguards, adequate notice, limited intervention prior to a full hearing, and limited application upon sufficient facts of an emergency and inability to consent. Such provisions are more consistent with the notions of constitutionally protected rights of due process and privacy. Critics of present legislation argue that this in and of itself is not sufficient. It is contended that despite such safeguards, there exists inherent weaknesses and potential of abuse in statutes that rely on terms such as "lacks the capacity to consent" without a clear, articulated definition. Medical and legal labels of incompetency and capacity in many cases express personal judgments on the conduct in question. Appropriate intervention can best be determined if <u>functional disability</u> can be identified. But this premise becomes less easily followed when viewed in terms of an infirm elderly person's "capacity" to consent to services or placement. So long as the statutes fail to address this issue, they leave the door open to inappropriate intervention.

The Uniform Probate Code attempts to address this problem,* but does not fully abandon the need to demonstrate a condition causing the functional incapacity. The Code defines an incapacitated person as one "who is impaired by reason of mental illness, mental deficiency, physical illness, mental deficiency, physical illness or disability, advanced age, chronic use of drugs, chronic intoxication, or other cause (except minority) to the extent that he lacks sufficient understanding or capacity to make or communicate responsible decisions concerning his person." Inability to engage in decision-making about matters affecting one's person is thus seen as the core of the functional disorder produced by a variety of conditions.

This formulation, however, introduces another complication. Physical illness and disability, not just mental condition, are recognized as causes of functional inability and therefore are logically included in the definition. The problem with this approach is that courts thereby are empowered to appoint guardians with important powers over the person and the estate of adults who are mentally competent, yet physically incapacitated. Thus, a court could sanction an involuntary guardianship for an elderly stroke victim who has lost the power to speak and write, but who is otherwise mentally fit. Moreover, the Uniform Probate Code definition refers to "responsible" decision-making, thereby allowing a court to evaluate the merits of particular decisions by physically disabled but mentally competent persons, and, if the court disagrees with them, to find the person incapacitated and appoint a guardian.

THE ROLE OF THE PUBLIC AGENCY

Most of the states provide for a "public guardianship," that is, court appointment of a

*See, Regan, John J.,"Protecting the Elderly: The New Paternalism,"Hastings Law Journal, May, 1981, 1111, from which this discussion is drawn.

public official or agency to implement a protective services order or to serve as guardian of an incompetent person, usually when no other private person or agency is available or willing to assume this responsibility. In Maryland, each county has a nine-member Disabled Persons Review Board which semi-annually reviews all public guardianships and recommends to the court the continuation, modification, or termination of the guardianship. Connecticut requires the public guardian to prepare written plans for services to the disabled client and to submit the plan to the regional ombudsman who has the right to comment on the proposal. None of the other jurisdictions provide for special oversight of their protective services agencies. Yet there always looms any number of problems which the legislation presently does not address itself to.

For example, there may be a conflict of interest between an agency's fiduciary responsibility to the client and its limited fiscal authority as a public body to provide the services needed by that client. The delegation of day-to-day guardianship duties to various caseworkers within an agency may depersonalize a guardianship and negate any real personal fiduciary role. A heavy caseload also may lead to the neglect of a client. As pointed out supra, thus far only the states of Maryland and Connecticut provide for methods of review.

LEAST RESTRICTIVE ALTERNATIVE

Most of the states that have adopted adult protective services legislation clearly state in the legislative intent provision that services provided should be the least restrictive alternative. This implies an acknowledgment of the state's obligation to provide care and protection with the least necessary restrictions on that person's liberty and civil rights. But as the discussion in the previous section notes, and as numerous commentators have pointed out, There are serious procedural flaws in the laws of some of the states, and lesser weaknesses in several others. The standards for intervention are essentially vague and conclusory. The intervenor, even a public agency, is rarely accountable to anyone, including the court, once the court has signed the order. Thus it is frequently charged that protective services, especially when provided by a public agency, are becoming in many states a mechanism to allow the public agency to assume total dominion over elderly clients. But these criticisms are based only on statutory analysis and do not take into account agency regulations and practice, which may very well impose controls not apparent in the statutes.

State legislatures will undoubtedly review their present laws which are relatively recent and untried. In time, legislation will approach the measure of effectiveness required for this increasingly large percentage of our population, the elderly. Until such time, however, advocates for the protection of the elderly who fall into life-threatening circumstances due to abuse and exploitation and neglect, must use the prevailing laws as effectively as possible.

Chapter 4
MANDATORY REPORTING LAWS
FOR ADULT ABUSE:
SUMMARY CHARTS*

Alabama

Date Passed: "Adult Protective Services Act of 1976"

Persons Covered: 18 and over, due to physical or mental impairment, cannot protect self from abuse, with no guardian or relative able and willing, whose behavior indicates he is mentally incompetent to care for self without serious consequences to self and others

Central Registry: Not provided for in law

Department Responsible
for Implementation: Department of Pensions and Security

Reports Sent to: County Department of Pensions and Security or Chief of Police or County Sheriff

Required Reporters: All physicians and other practitioners of healing arts

Penalty for Failure
to Report: Guilty of misdemeanor; fine of 500 dollars or less or 6 months or less

Penalty for Caretaker
Maltreatment: Guilty of misdemeanor; fine of 500 dollars or less or 6 months or less or both

Payment Provisions: Department is not chargeable for the costs of care, except where

---

*Source citation appears on p. 82

such care is specifically provided
for by law, or if Department regulations and funding exist for such
purposes. If person is eligible
for service programs of Department,
follow usual Departmental policies;
if he is ineligible for Department
services other than protective services he is to make payment for
services

Mandated Time Period
  for Investigation
of Report: Agency receiving report must investi-
            gate within 3 days; law enforcement
            must forward reports received to
            County Department of Pensions and
            Security within 24 hours

Case Review Mechanisms: After protective place-
            ment, Department gives written re-
            port to court at least once every
            6 months

Voluntary Service
  Provision: All protective services shall be
            in conformity with wishes of person
            to be served, unless the person is
            unable or unwilling to accept such
            services; in that case the court
            can order them. Department is re-
            quired to provide services only
            for persons it is equipped to serve
            and agrees to serve

Provision to Enter
  and Investigate: Not provided for in law

Provision to Enjoin
  Caretaker from
Interfering: Not provided for in law

Provision for Guardian-
  ship, Conservatorship: -A guardian may be ap-
            pointed by the court
            -Other than for the limited pur-

42

pose of transporting for protective placement, the Department should not be appointed guardian or custodian,
-If agreeable with person, court can appoint a guardian having the same powers as a guardian of a person of unsound mind (it is not necessary to hold sanity hearing).
-If adult needs protective services and is unable to manage estate, an interested person may petition the court to preserve the estate and direct use of it for person's needs.

Involuntary or Emergency
Service Provision: If person does not consent or is incapable of consent, Department can petition court for services; if it is urgently necessary to protect person's health, court may order protective placement. Any interested person may petition court for protective placement; court appoints hearing date within 30 days of petition filing; court appoints guardian ad litem if person has no counsel at hearing; court should follow individual preference for non-institutional care whenever possible.

Due Process Safeguards: -Protective services should allow individual same rights as other citizens
-Services should be designed to place least possible restriction on person's liberty and constitutional rights, consistent with due process
-In involuntary protective placement, court should give notice to others within 10 days of this action, on the person's location, etc. and set time for hearing on need

for present placement; jury of
6 persons is impanelled to try the
facts
-Person cannot be committed to men-
talhealth facility under the act
-No civil rights are relinquished
as a result of protective placement; cannot give medical care if
person objects on basis of conflict
with religious beliefs
-"As far as is compatible with mental and physical condition of adult,
every reasonable effort should be
made to assure no action's taken
without full and informed consent
of person."

Arkansas

Date Passed: Arkansas Statutes 59-1301-Act 166 of 1977, "Adult Protective Services Act"

Persons Covered: 18 and over, persons suffering from developmental disabilities, the infirmities of aging or other like incapacities

Central Registry: A statewide Central Registry to be established in Department, and state-wide toll-free telephone number for reports. (Registry includes treatment plan, case disposition)

Department Responsible for
Implementation: Department of Human Services

Reports Sent to: Department of Human Services

Required Reporters: Wide variety of professionals (doctors, nurses, hospital personnel, social workers, mental health professionals, peace officers, employees of public and private facilities);
-any other person may report

Penalty for Failure
to Report: Guilty of misdemeanor

Penalty for Caretakers'
Maltreatment: Guilty of felony, lessor neglect guilty of misdemeanor

Payment Provisions: No specific provisions

Mandated Time Period
for Investigation
of Report: Receiving agency should forward report to Central Registry and to appropriate law enforcement agency;

investigation must include home
visit

Care Review Mechanisms: Department to make written reports and case summary to
state Central Registry. Reports
into Central Registry should be
sent to Adult Protective Services
immediately

Voluntary Service
  Provision: Protective services include evaluation of need, arrangements for
appropriate living quarters, securing medical and legal services,
obtaining financial benefits. Any
person may request voluntary protective placement, without relin-
quishing his civil rights

Provision to Enter
  and Investigate: Probate court can order entry
into home

Provision to Enjoin
  Caretaker from
Interfering: Not provided for in law

Provision for Guardianship,
  Conservatorship: No specific provisions

Involuntary or Emergency
  Service Provision: If there is imminent
danger to adult's life or health,
temporary protective custody can
be arranged, not to exceed 72
hours; probate court and Department shall be notified in order
to initiate adult protective proceedings; certain persons or officials are authorized to take
adult into temporary protective
custody (police, person in charge
of institution, agency employee
can arrange it); if good cause
shown, probate court can issue

46

order for temporary protective custody; person authorized in law to take person into custody may petition court to provide long term protective custody.

Due Process Safeguards: If temporary protective order is used, hold hearing within 48 hours to establish probable cause for grounds for protective custody. Upon this finding, temporary protective custody can be ordered for up to 14 days, pending hearing for long term protective custody. If long term protective custody order is issued: Notice must be served on person at least 10 days prior to hearing
-Court should decide according to least drastic alternative, including finding for non-institutional care whenever possible
-Person cannot be committed to mental asylum, unless in best interests
-Court should review status of case at least every 6 months, from admission date
-Person can appeal a long term protective custody commitment

Connecticut

Date Passed: Public Act /77-613, "Act Adopting
a Reporting Law for Protection of
the Elderly"

Persons Covered: 60 and over

Central Registry: Each Regional Ombudsman main-
tains a registry and forwards it
to Department on Aging for State-
wide registry (includes reports,
evaluations and recommendations)

Department Responsible
  for Implementation: Department of Aging

Required Reporters: Wide variety of professionals (doctors, nurses, employees of
nursing homes, medical examiners,
chiropractors, podiatrists, social
workers, coroners, clergy, police,
pharmacists); any other person
may report; report within 5 calendar days

Penalty for Failure
  to Report: Fine of 500 dollars or less

Penalty for Caretaker
  Maltreatment: Not provided in law

Payment Provisions: -If financially able, elder
should pay for services
-50,000 dollars appropriated to
Department of Social Services
-Department on Aging shall reim-
burse general fund for any amounts
expended from funds appropriated
to Department of Social Services
for act

Mandated Time Period
  for Investigation of
Report: Prompt evaluation of report, including
home visit (by Regional Ombudsman)

48

Case Review Mechanisms: Department of Social Services treatment plan to Regional Ombudsman within 10 days of report receipt; after service authorization, Department re-evaluates case every 90 days

Voluntary Service Provision: If protective services deemed necessary, Regional Ombudsman refers case to Department of Social Services for service provision, assuming client assents.
-If client does not consent or withdraws consent, services must stop, unless Commissioner believes client lacks the capacity to consent, in which case he can seek court intervention

Provision to Enter and Investigate: Not provided for in law

Provision to Enjoin Caretaker from Interfering: Social Service Commissioner may petition court for order enjoining caretaker from interfering with service provision to which elder consents

Provision for Guardianship, Conservatorship: If person fails to consent to services, and Regional Ombudsman has reason to believe he lacks "capacity to consent", he refers case to Department to determine whether to file petition to appoint conservator; probate court may appoint Commissioner of Social Services Department as conservator

Involuntary or Emergency Service Provision: No specific provision

Due Process Safeguards: If Department petitions

court to appoint conservator for
elder lacking capacity to consent,
elder can motion to review court's
determination or any order issued
pursuant to act; elder has the right
to an attorney

Florida

Date Passed: Florida Statutes, Chapter 827.09, "Developmentally Disabled Abused Act," passed 1973, amended 1980 to include elderly

Florida Statutes S-409-3631 *et seq*, Chapters 77-336, "Adult Protective Services Act", passed 1977

Persons Covered: Disabled persons and those suffering from infirmities of aging

Central Registry: In Department of Health and Rehabilitation, modeled after child abuse registry (record investigation results)

Department Responsible
for Implementation: Department of Health and Rehabilitation Services

Reports Sent to: Department of Health and Rehabilitation Services

Required Reporters: Professionals and lay (doctors, nurses, psychologists, teachers, social workers, employees of private and public facilities)

Failure to Report: Guilty of misdemeanor

Penalty for Caretaker
Maltreatment: Not provided for in law

Payment Provisions: Department authorized to make advances for program start-up or to make periodic advance payments

Mandated Time Period
for Investigation of
Report: Immediately

<u>Case Review Mechanisms</u>: After determination of probable cause, Department should notify appropriate human rights advocate committee of alleged abuse

<u>Voluntary Service Provision</u>: Department has the right to authorize transfer of elder from nursing home

<u>Provision to Enter and Investigate</u>: Not provided for in this law

<u>Provision to Enjoin Caretaker from Interfering</u>: Not provided for in this law

<u>Involuntary or Emergency Service Provision</u>: Not provided for in this law

<u>Due Process Safeguards</u>: No specific provisions in this law

52

Kentucky

Date Passed: Kentucky Revised Statutes,209,
"Kentucky Adult Protection Act".
passed 1976, amended 1978 and 1980

Persons Covered: 18 and over (or married person
without regard to age), who, due
to mental or physical dysfunctioning, or, who is victim of spouse
abuse, cannot manage own resources
or protect self, and has no one
willing to assist him/her

Central Registry: Not provided for in law

Department Responsible
for Implementation: Department of Human Resources

Reports Sent to: Department of Human Resources

Required Reporters: Any person, including but
not limited to law enforcement
officer, nurse, social worker,
coroner, medical examiner, alternate care facility employee; death
of adult does not relieve reporter
of responsibility

Payment Provisions: If need exists, Department
will provide services, within
budgetary limitations; guardian
ad litem fee, if appointed, to be
paid by Department and not to exceed 300 dollars

Mandated Time Period
for Investigation of
Report: As soon as possible; appropriate law
enforcement agency should also be notified

Case Review Mechanisms: Written report and recommendations; after emergency protective services provision, Department

reports to court once a month

Voluntary Service
  Provision: Intent is to authorize only the
            least possible restriction on ex-
            ercise of personal and civil rights,
            consistent with need for services
            and person's safety and welfare

Provision to Enter
  and Investigate: Search warrant may be issued
            if adult or caretaker does not
            consent to investigation; any De-
            partmental representative may enter
            licensed health facility

Provision to Enjoin
  Caretaker from
Interfering: Court may issue restraining order
            or other injunctive relief to pro-
            hibit any violation of chapter

Provision for Guardianship,
  Conservatorship: When court petition for emer-
            gency protective services is filed,
            court shall immediately appoint a
            guardian ad litem to represent adult,
            interview him and counsel on rights

Involuntary or Emergency
  Service Provision: Court may order services
            on an emergency basis if adult
            lacks capacity to consent to ser-
            vices, it is an emergency, and he
            is abused; court may order protec-
            tive services if person lacks capac-
            ity to consent or if he refuses
            and no one else is authorized to
            consent by law

Due Process Safeguards: -Intent is to require
            that due process be followed
            -After petition for emergency pro-
            tective service is filed-issue
            summons and serve adult and care-

taker with copy, at least 3 days
prior to hearing
-At hearing, adult may present evidence, cross-examine, petition to
have order set aside

Minnesota

Date Passed: MSA 626,557 *et seq*, "Reporting
of Maltreatment of Vulnerable
Adults", effective 1981

Persons Covered: 18 and over, vulnerable adults
who, regardless of residence, are
unable or unlikely to report abuse
or neglect without assistance due
to impaired physical or mental or
emotional status

Central Registry: Not provided for in law

Department Responsible
  for Implementation: State Welfare Department

Reports Sent to: Local Police Department,
county sheriff, local welfare
agency or appropriate licensing
agency

Required Reporters: Professionals caring for
vulnerable adults (educators,
law enforcement, employees in facilities); a person not required
to report may voluntarily report
if required reporter suspects direct or indirect death from abuse,
he should report to medical examiner or coroner, who does exam
and reports to police and welfare
departments

Penalty for Failure
  to Report: Guilty of dismeanor

Penalty for Caretaker
  Maltreatment: Not provided in law

Payment Provisions: 113,000 dollars appropriated
from general fund to Commissioner
of Public Welfare and is available
to June, 1981

Mandated Time Period
  for Investigation: Immediately; offer emergency
and continuing protective services;
upon receipt of report, police department should notify local welfare agency; welfare agency, upon
receipt of report, should notify
police and appropriate licensing
agencies

Case Review Mechanisms: Agency should keep appropriate records

Voluntary Service
  Provision: If abuse occurred in licensed
facility, welfare agency should
immediately notify licensing
agency of suspected abuse; licensing agency should investigate
immediately, enter facilities;
each facility should have Abuse
Prevention Plan

Provision to Enter
  and Investigate: Local welfare agencies have
right to enter facilities and in-
spect records

Provision to Enjoin
  Caretaker from
Interfering: Not provided for in law

Provision for Guardianship,
  Conservatorship: No specific provisions

Involuntary or Emergency
  Service Provision: When necessary to prevent
further harm, agency shall seek
authority to remove adult from
caretakers; also determine if other
adults are in jeopardy and offer
protective services

Due Process Safeguards: No specific provisions

Missouri

Date Passed: Senate Bill /576; effective 1981

Persons Covered: 60 and over, unable to protect own interests or care for themselves

Central Registry: Department to maintain statewide toll-free number for receipt of reports

Department Responsible
for Implementation: Department of Social Services

Reports Sent to: Department of Social Services, Division of Aging

Required Reports: Any person

Penalty for Failure
to Report: Not provided for in law

Penalty for Catetaker
Maltreatment: Not provided for in law

Payment Provisions: No specific provisions

Mandated Time Period
for Investigation
of Report: Prompt and Thorough investigation by Department of Social Services

Case Review Mechanisms: No specific provisions

Voluntary Service
Provision: Department provides social casework and counseling assistance in provision of services; services must stop if adult refuses or withdraws consent, unless Director has reasonable cause to believe he lacks the capacity to consent, then he may seek court order; if adult consents to services, they should

58

be arranged by Department, in
least restrictive environment
available

Provision to enter
and Investigate:
Department can petition
court for warrant to enter premises and investigate, if any person bars access to investigation
by Department

Provision to Enjoin
Caretaker from
Interfering:
Director may seek court order to
enjoin person barring access from
interfering with investigation

Provision for Guardianship,
Conservatorship:
If court finds an adult incompetent, it can appoint a
guardian; if guardian refuses to
consent to services, and person
cannot consent due to incompetency
or legal disability and danger of
serious physical harm is likely,
court can take such action as
necessary

Involuntary or Emergency
Service Provision:
If person lacks capacity
to consent, and is in danger of
serious physical harm, peace officer may transport adult to medical facility, he may also get
court warrant to enter premises
and remove adult; Director of medical facility can get court order
to treat adult

Due Process Safeguards:
Person cannot be com-
mitted to mental health facility
under act

Nebraska

Date Passed: LB505, "Child Protective Act of 1979", as amended in 1979

Persons Covered: Children, Incompetent or disabled persons

Central Registry: A Central Register of child protection cases maintained by Department; Department of Public Welfare to file each report of suspected abuse or neglect in a special state Abused or Neglected Child, Incompetent or Disabled Person Registry; Single state-wide toll-free number within Department (24 hours-day, 7 days-week)

Department Responsible
for Implementation: Department of Public Welfare, or proper law enforcement agency

Reports Sent to: Department of Public Welfare or law enforcement agency

Required Reporters: Any physician, medical institution, nurse, school employee, social worker or any other person

Penalty for Failure
to Report: Or release of confidential information guilty of misdemeanor

Penalty for Caretaker
Maltreatment: Not provided in law

Payment Provisions: No specific provisions

Mandated Time Period
for Investigation of
Report: Any reports received by Department, also report to law enforcement agency; upon receipt of any report by law enforcement agency, it is duty to

60

determine whether investigation
deemed warranted; if so, to do it
immediately-- institute legal proceedings if appropriate; law enforcement to notify Department if
investigation undertaken (on next
business day after receipt of report); Division shall investigate
each case referred by Department,
provide social services necessary
to protect person and preserve
family; law enforcement agencies
receiving report to notify state
central registry, next working
day; Division may request further
help from law enforcement agency
or take such legal action as appropriate

Case Review Mechanisms: Division shall make
written report or case summary,
as Department may require, to proper law enforcement agency in the
county and to the state registry
of all reported cases

Voluntary Service Provision: No specific provision

Provision to Enter and
Investigate: Not provided for in law

Provision to Enjoin
Caretaker from
Interfering: Not provided for in law

Provision for Guardianship,
Conservatorship: No specific provisions

Involuntary or Emergency
Service Provision: No specific provisions

Due Process Safeguards: No specific provisions

New Hampshire

Date Passed: State Law RSA 161-D, "Protective Services to Adults", passed 1977

Persons Covered: 18 and over, found to manifest a degree of incapacity by reason of limited mental or physical function which may result in harm or hazard to self or others, or who cannot manage own estate

Central Registry: To be established at Division of Welfare (keep information on every case)

Department Responsible
for Implementation: Division of Welfare, Department of Health and Welfare

Reports Sent to: Division of Welfare (if after working hours report to police department or county sheriff)

Required Reporters: All physicians and other practitioners of healing arts

Penalty for Failure
to Report: Guilty of misdemeanor

Penalty for Caretaker
Maltreatment: Not provided for in law

Payment Provisions: No specific provisions

Mandated Time Period for
Investigation of Report: Director shall investigate within 72 hours of report receipt; law enforcement should notify Department of Health and Welfare within 72 hours of report receipt

Case Review Mechanisms: No specific provisions

Voluntary Service Provision: Protective ser-

vices shall include guidance,
counseling; when necessary, assistance in securing safe and sani-
tary living accommodations, and
mental and physical examinations

**Provision to Enter
and Investigate:** Upon finding of probable
cause, probate court can order
police officer, probation officer
or social worker to enter premises
to investigate, if the adult or
the caretaker refuses to allow
Department representative to investigate

**Provision to Enjoin
Caretaker from
Interfering:** Not provided for in law

**Provision for Guardianship,
Conservatorship:** If all other remedies are
exhausted, Director or authorized
guardian may act to have guardian
or conservator appointed by probate court, pursuant to RSA 464,
for any adult in need of protective services

**Involuntary or Emergency
Service Provision:** No specific provisions

Due Process Safeguards: Protective services
shall not include commitment to
state hospital or school; probate
court may order proposed ward to
submit to medical or psychiatric
exam, to be completed within 30
days, court gets written report.
If proposed ward objects to the
evaluation, probate court should
be notified within 5 days after
notification of evaluation's time
and place, and hold hearing to
consider objection before ordering evaluation

North Carolina

<u>Date Passed</u>: "Protection of the Abused, Neglected or Exploited Disabled Adult Act", effective 1974, amended 1976 to cover 18 and up

<u>Persons Covered</u>: 18 and over, disabled adults or anyone physically or mentally incapacitated due to advanced age, conditions incurred at any age

<u>Central Registry</u>: Not provided for in law

<u>Department Responsible for Implementation</u>: Department of Social Services

<u>Reports Sent to</u>: Department of Social Services

<u>Required Reporters</u>: Any person with reason to believe

<u>Penalty for Failure to Report</u>: Not provided for in law

<u>Penalty for Caretaker Maltreatment</u>: Not provided for in law

<u>Payment Provisions</u>: Any funds for protective services system may be matched by state and federal funds, to be utilized by County Department of Social Services; if individual is financially able to pay, he should; if not, services are free

<u>Mandated Time Period for Investigation of Report</u>: Prompt and thorough investigation, including home visit then written report

<u>Case Review Mechanisms</u>: Department should adopt standards within 90 days to implement act

Voluntary Service
Provision: If adult consents, service provision can start; if he does not consent or withdraws consent, services must stop unless Department determines individual lacks capacity to consent; it can then petition court to order services

Provision to Enter
and Investigate: Not provided for in law

Provision to Enjoin
Caretaker from
Interfering: Department can petition court for order enjoining caretaker interference; if need is there, person consents to services, and caretaker does not

Provision for Guardianship,
Conservatorship: Court order may include appointing individual to be responsible for service provision; within 60 days of appointment, court reviews case to determine if petition be initiated

Involuntary or Emergency
Service Provision: Department may petition court to order emergency services if the person lacks the capacity to consent, and emergency exists, person needs protective services, and no one else is able or willing to consent to services
-emergency services may include physical custody
-court shall hold hearing within 14 days of petition filing

Due Process Safeguards: In petition for emergency intervention, must give notice to person or spouse or guardian at least 24 hours prior to hearing on petition, unless

court determines death or irreparable harm will result from delay

-In emergency court order, only order services necessary to remove the emergency

-Disabled adult must receive at least 5 days notice of hearing; has right to be present, to counsel (if indigent, state bears cost of counsel; court can appoint guardian ad litem if he lacks capacity to waive right to counsel

Oklahoma

Date Passed: Title 43A of Oklahoma Statutes, sections 801-810, "Protective Services for the Elderly Act," passed 1977

Persons Covered: 65 and over (amended from 70 and over effective 1980)

Central Registry: Not provided for in law

Department Responsible
  for Implementation: Department of Institutions, Social and Rehabilitative Services

Reports sent to: Department of Institutions

Required Reporters: Any person

Penalty for Failure
  to Report: Not provided for in law

Penalty for Caretaker
  Maltreatment: Not provided for in law

Payment Provisions: Costs of protective services to be borne by Department, unless person agrees to pay, or Department determines he can pay

Mandated Time Period for
  Investigation of Report: Prompt and thorough, diagnostic evaluation home visit consultation with others

Case Review Mechanisms: No specific provisions

Voluntary Service
  Provision: If person does not consent or withdraws consent, services stop, unless the Department determines person lacks capacity to consent, then it can seek court authorization

**Provision to Enter
and Investigate:** Department may petition
court for entry into home; Department representative should go with
peace officer; in an emergency
order, court may authorize forced
entry to premises, to give services
or transport elsewhere (peace officer accompanies Department representative)

**Provision to Enjoin
Caretaker from
Interfering:** Department can petition court for
order to enjoin caretaker interference

**Provision for Guardianship,
Conservatorship:** In an emergency order, court
appoints Department or a person
as temporary guardian of the person, with responsibility to consent to services; if person still
needs services after one renewal
of temporary order, court can appoint guardian and/or apply for
commitment to nursing home or other
placement

**Involuntary or Emergency
Service Provision:** If person lacks capacity
to consent, court may order involuntary services through emergency order; if adult is in substantial risk of death or immediate
harm to self, lacks capacity to
consent, and no consent can be obtained.
- emergency services may be provided for 72 hour period, upon
proper showing
- court can authorize continued
involuntary protective services
for 6 months or less, when the
order for continued involuntary
protective services expires,

guardian or anyone else can petition court to extend order, not to
exceed 6 months; emergency placement may be made to nursing home,
foster care, but not to mental
hospitals

Due Process Safeguards: -Anyone may petition
to set aside court order
-Protective services shall, to the
maximum degree of flexibility,
guarantee the individual the same
rights as other citizens; give
least restrictive services; court
should only authorize least restrictive intervention, consistent
with welfare and liberty, attempt
to maintain person at home or in
present living situation
-In petition for emergency services, person must receive 48
hours notice of hearing, unless
it is a situation of extreme danger;
person has right to be present, to
counsel

South Carolina

Date Passed: Adult Protective Services Law, "Protective Services for Developmentally Disabled and Senile Persons," amended 1976 and 1979 (Act 1082 of 1974)

Persons Covered: 18 and over, senile, developmentally disabled, mentally ill

Central Registry: Not provided for in law

Department Responsible
  for Implementation: Department of Social Services

Reports Sent to: County Department of Social Services or sheriff or law enforcement

Required Reporters: All practitioners of the healing arts

Failure to Report: Charged as accessory after fact and guilty of misdemeanor upon conviction shall be fined not less than 100 dollars nor more than 1000 dollars or be imprisoned for not more than 6 months; penalty for violating provisions of chapter guilty of misdemeanor, and upon conviction fined 500 dollars or less or 90 days in jail or less

Penalty for Caretaker
  Maltreatment: Unlawful to abuse, neglect, or exploit-guilty of misdemeanor upon conviction-fined not less than 500 dollars nor more than 5000 dollars, or be imprisoned for not less than 90 days nor more than 5 years

<u>Payment Provisions</u>: Reasonable expenses required
by chapter shall be borne by De-
partment. Department shall seek
appropriate federal reimbursement
for such evaluations

<u>Mandated Time Period</u>
<u> for Investigation</u>
<u>of Report</u>: Investigation within 3 days; re-
ports by sheriff or law enforce-
ment must be forwarded to County
Social Service Department within
24 hours

<u>Case Review Mechanisms</u>: Department which accepts
a protective placement should make
written evaluation and report at
least once every 6 months on client's
mental, physical, and social condition

<u>Voluntary Service</u>
<u> Provision</u>: Protective services shall include
arrangement for living quarters,
obtaining financial benefits, securing medical and legal services;
all protective services shall be
voluntary unless ordered by the
court or requested by a parent,
guardian or friend; any interested
person may request service on behalf of another

<u>Provision to Enter</u>
<u> and Investigate</u>: Not provided for in law

<u>Provision to Enjoin</u>
<u>Caretaker from</u>
<u>Interfering</u>: Not provided for in law

<u>Provision for Guardian-</u>
<u> ship, Conservatorship</u>: -In protective place-
ment order, court shall appoint
guardian ad litem for person
-Before expiration of 90 day period,
proper hearing shall be held to

71

determine if further care is required

Service Provision: Department, agency or guardian can request family or other court to provide protective placement for care or custody of individual, it cannot be ordered unless court determines individual is unable to provide for own protection from abuse or neglect by another or self; in protective placement, if court decides such agency care is urgently needed, Department can assume custody, upon court order, and place person in facility for period not exceeding 90 days; use Department resources to provide suitable permanent environment; with consent of person in custody, care period can go beyond 90 days; pending trial of any case, Department is authorized to provide protective services; if conviction results, agency may continue such services till suitable permanent arrangements are made; court can provide such legal protection necessary to care for person; if person is unable to care for self due to physical, mental disability or financial resources, agency can immediately provide care to extent person is not taken into custody or removed from home, or agency can petition court for temporary order authorizing agency to take custody and provide care till suitable permanent arrangements are made; prior to discharge from custody of Department, Department shall review need for continued protective service, including appointment of guardian or limited

guardian; court can appoint such
a guardian, upon Department's recommendations; at court hearing to
get temporary custody order, any
interested person can join or op-
pose the petition, but notice to
such interested person is not required

Due Process Safeguards: Protective services shall
allow person same rights as other
citizens, while protecting from
abuse, neglect, and exploitation;
services should place the least
possible restriction on personal
liberty and the exercise of constitutional rights; court should
follow least drastic alternative,
including preference for non-
institutional care whenever possible;
no civil rights relinquished when
person requests voluntary protective placement

Tennesse

Date Passed: "Adult Protection Act" passed
1978, amended 1980 (1980 amendment
to 1978 law repealed the previous
1974 law) "Protective Services for
the Elderly" (mandated protective
services for 60 and up)

Persons Covered: 18 and over, who because of
physical or mental dysfunctioning
or advanced age (60 or above) is
unable to manage own resources,
carry out daily living, or protect self from abuse without help
from others and no one available
to assist

Central Registry: Not provided for in law

Department Responsible
for Implementation: Department of Human Services

Reports Sent to: Department of Human Services

Required Reporters: Any person including, but
not limited to M.D., nurse, social
worker, Department personnel,
coroner, alternate care facility
employee or caretaker; death of
adult does not relieve one of responsibility for reporting, however unless report indicates other
adults are in similar situation
and need protection, it shall not
be necessary for Department to
make investigation of circumstances
regarding death, provided proper
law enforcement officials are notified

Penalty for Failure
to Report: Guilty of misdemeanor, fined not
more than 50 dollars or imprisoned
not more than 3 months, or both

74

<u>Penalty for Caretaker</u>
  <u>Maltreatment</u>: Not provided for in law

<u>Payment Provisions</u>: If Department determines pro-
                    tective services are necessary, it
                    has authority to provide them with-
                    in budgetary limitations and avail-
                    ability of funds, except where
                    adult refuses services; if Depart-
                    ment determined adult can pay, a-
                    dult shall reimburse state for
                    cost of protective services; if
                    not state bears cost; otherwise
                    Department can recover such cost
                    from adult in any court; cost of
                    administration of chapter and pro-
                    vision of shall be limited to
                    amount of funds specifically ap-
                    propriated for such purposes by
                    general assembly

<u>Mandated Time Period</u>
  <u>for Investigation</u>
<u>of Report</u>: Upon receipt of report Department shall
            as soon as practical:
            1-notify appropriate law enforce-
              ment agency
            2-make an investigation of complaint
            3-written report of findings and
              recommendations
            4-notify reporter of its deter-
              mination
            5-any Department representative
              may enter any health facility
              licensed by state to carry out
              chapter's provisions
            6-any Department representative
              may, with adult's consent, enter
              any private premises where al-
              leged victim is to investigate
             -Investigation shall include a
            personal interview
             -Where abuse or neglect is al-
            legedly cause of death, coroner's
            or M.D.'s report shall be explained
            as part of investigation

75

Case Review Mechanisms: Department may adopt
                       such rules as are necessary

Voluntary Service
  Provision: Protective services can include
             investigation, procurement of
             suitable care in or out of home,
             legal determination of abuse, ne-
             glect or exploitation; if adult
             does not consent or withdraws con-
             sent to services, services shall
             be terminated, unless Department
             determines he lacks capacity to
             consent, in which case it may
             seek court authorization to pro-
             vide protective services; if adult
             elects to accept protective ser-
             vices, caretaker shall not inter-
             fere with provision of services;
             if, as result of investigation,
             Department determines adult who is
             resident of facility owned or op-
             erated by administrative depart-
             ment of state is in need of pro-
             tective services, department shall
             make report of investigation, to
             Commissioner with responsibility
             for facility, then it is responsi-
             bility of that Commissioner and
             not Department of Human Services
             to protect person

Provision to Enter
  and Investigate: If adult or caretaker does
             not consent to investigation of
             private premises of alleged vic-
             tim, search warrant may be issued
             upon showing of probable cause

Provision to Enjoin
  Caretaker from
Interfering: Any Chancery court, upon proper
             application by Department, may
             issue a temporary restraining or-
             der or other injunctive relief to
             prohibit any violation of this

76

chapter, regardless of existence
of any other remedy at law

Provision for Guardian-
ship, Conservatorship:
Any individual or organ-
ization appointed responsible for
personal welfare of adult, has only
specific authority granted in court
order, to consent to specific protective services and appropriate
custodial care if ordered; if adult
needs person to manage his other
affairs, appoint a Limited guardian
according to Conservatorship Law
of 1980; Department is not required
to initiate proceedings for Limited
Guardian to assume such duties

Involuntary or Emergency
Service Provision:
If Department determines
adult is in need of protective
services, is in imminent danger of
death, and lack capacity to consent
to services, then Department may
file complaint with court for order
authorizing protective services
necessary to prevent death; order
may designate individual or organization to be responsible for welfare of adult; within 5 days of
entering order, court should hold
hearing on merits, if hearing is
not held, order is dissolved; if
Department determines adult lacks
capacity to consent and needs protective services, it can petition
court for hearing; adult must get
at least 10 day notice of hearing,
has right to be present, to counsel;
court order authorizing services
may include designating person or
organization responsible for welfare of adult; emergency protective services may include taking
adult into physical custody in
home or in medical or nursing

facility, if court finds this is
necessary to prevent imminent death;
if court orders this, Department
shall review decree annually

Due Process Safeguards: Adult must receive at
least 48 hours notice of hearing
on protective services; has right
to be present, to be represented
by counsel; state will bear cost
of counsel if adult is indigent;
no adult may be committed to
mental institution or adjudicated
incompetent under chapter; see
provisions under "Emergency Service Provision"

Utah

Date Passed: HB No. 125, "Adult Prorective Services", passed 1977

Persons Covered: 18 and over, disabled adults who are incapacitated due to mental retardation, physical conditions, infirmities of aging or other like incapacities whose condition prevents them from providing for own care and protection

Central Registry: Not provided for in law

Department Responsible
  for Implementation: Division of Family Services

Reports Sent to: Local police or county sheriff

Required Reporters: Any person, including but not limited to M.D., social worker, psychologist, nurse, teacher, employee of facility

Penalty for Failure
  to Report: Not provided for in law

Penalty for Caretaker
  Maltreatment: Guilty of felony

Payment Provisions: Costs incurred to be borne by Division of Family Services, unless court appoints guardian and costs are paid from the estate, or another government agency pays for eligible services

Mandated Time Period
  for Investigation
of Report: No specific provisions

Case Review Mechanisms: Division shall institute procedures to implement act, including guidelines for initiation of

79

guardianship proceedings, referral
to the public guardian, and designation of the facilities for protective placement

Voluntary Service
Provision: Intervention shall be consistent
with the preferred life style of
the adult; protective services
should be voluntary, unless court
ordered

Provision to Enter
and Investigate: Not provided for in law

Provision to Enjoin
Caretaker from
Interfering: Division may petition court for
decree enjoining caretaker from
interfering with service provision,
if the person consents or lacks
capacity to consent to services,
if he needs services, and the
caretaker interferes

Provision for Guardian-
ship, Conservatorship: Department may be appointed by court as trustee, receiver or guardian over person,
estate, or both, pertinent to
provisions of Utah Probate Code

Involuntary or Emergency
Service Provision: If disabled adult fails
to consent to adult protective
services, or if consent is withdrawn, or if the Division determines the adult lacks the capacity
to consent, Division may petition
court for authorization to provide
protective services; if court
finds adult lacks capacity to
consent, and needs protective
services, it issues order authorizing services by Division

<u>Due Process Safeguards</u>: Person given services
has right to:
- hearing on the petition and its
consequences (at least 10 days
notice of hearing)
- to be present at the hearing or
have interview by court, if
physically unable
- right to counsel, at every stage
of protective services; if poor,
court will appoint one
- right to offer evidence on own
behalf, to cross-examine witnesses
- right to written statement of
reason for protective order
- right to least possible restriction
on civil rights, consistent with
adult's welfare and safety (after
comprehensive assessment is made)
- any party may move for review of
court decree at any time

The following is a summary of provisions not
included in the above chart of laws:

Immunity

The reporting statutes guarantee reporters
immunity from civil and/or criminal liability
which might otherwise be incurred from participation in a report or judicial proceedings resulting from a report. Certain statutes
specifically include in the immunity coverage representatives of the department responsible for receiving and investigating reports.

Report Contents

All of the reporting statutes specify that a
report of abuse, neglect or exploitation include such identifying information as the
names and addresses of the alleged victim
and perpetrator, the nature and extent of

maltreatment, and any other information
relevant to the case. Some of the statutes
specify an oral or written report by the
reported; other statutes direct that an oral
report be followed by a written one.

Confidentiality

The majority of the reporting statutes include provisions for protecting the confidentiality of reports and the identity of persons involved. In particular, statutes establishing a Central Registry specify procedures
for maintaining the confidentiality of case
records, expunging unfounded reports and
authorizing access to records.

Privileged Information

Several of the reporting statutes stipulate
that no common law or statutory privilege
except the attorney-client privilege shall
apply in judicial proceedings resulting from
a case of abuse, neglect or exploitation.
Privileges for confidential communications
that are excluded in the statutes include
husband-wife, physician-patient and clergy-
client privileges.

Source Note: This material is reproduced from a
report by E. Salend, M. Satz, and
J. Pynoos of the UCLA-USC Long Term
Care Gerontology Center, prepared
for the National Conference on
Elder Abuse.

BIBLIOGRAPHY

Aging. Special issue on crime and the elderly,
1978.

Bane, M.J. Here to Stay: American Families
in the Twentieth Century. New York: Basic
Books, 1976.

"Battered Families: A Growing Nightmare."U.S.
News & World Report, January 15, 1979, 60-61.

Beattie, W.M. Jr."Aging and the Social Services."
In R.H. Binstock and E. Shanas, Handbook of
Aging and the Social Sciences, New York:
Van Nostrand Reinfold Co., 1976.

Bell, B.D., and Stanfield, G.G."The Aging
Stereotype in Experimental Perspective"
Gerontologist, 1973, 13, 341-344.

Bennett, R., and Eckman, J."Attitudes Toward
Aging: A Critical Examination of Recent
Literature and Implications for Future
Research."In C. Eisdorfer and M.P. Lawton,
(Eds.), The Psychology of Adult Development
and Aging. Washington, D.C. APA 1973.

Blau, Z.S."Changes in Status and Age Identification."American Sociological Review,
1956, 21, 198-201.

Blenkner, N."Social Work and Family Relation-
ships in Later Life with Some Thoughts on
Filial Maturity."In E. Shanas and G. Streib
(Eds.), Social Structure and the Family:
Generational Relations, Englewood Cliffs,
New Jersey: Prentice Hall, 1965.

Bloom, M. and Nielsen, M."The Older Person

in Need of Protective Services."Social Casework, 1971, 52(8), 500-509.

Briley, M."Battered Parents."Dynamic Years, 1979 (January-February), 14(2) 24-27.

Brostoff, P.M., Brown, R.B., and Butler, R.N. The Public Interest: Report No. 6. Beating Up the Elderly, 1972, 3(4) 319-322.

Brot, S."Neglected Elderly in Eastern Missouri." St. Louis Missouri Association for Prevention of Adult Abuse, 1979.

Burston, G.R."Do Your Elderly Parents Live in Fear of Being Battered?"Modern Geriatrics, November 16, 1978.
_____. Granny-battering. British Medical Journal, September 6, 1975, 3 (5983), 592.

Butler, R.N."The Effect of Medical and Health Progress on the Social and Economic Aspects of the Life Cycle."Industrial Gerontology, 1969, 2, 1-9.

Butler, R.N. and Lewis, M.I. Aging and Mental Health: Positive Psychosocial Approaches. St. Louis: C.V. Mosby & Co., 1973.

Butler, R.N. Why Survive? Being Old in America. New York: Harper & Row, 1974.

Clark, M."The Anthropology of Aging: A New Area for Studies of Culture and Personality." Gerontologist, 1967, 7, 55-64.

Clemente, F. and Kleiman, M.B."Fear of Crime Among the Aged."The Gerontologist, 1976, 16(3).

DeBeauvoir, S. The Coming of Age. New York: G.P. Putnam, 1973.

Drevenstedt, J. and Banziger, G. "Attitudes Toward the Elderly and Toward the Mentally

Ill. _Pschological Reports_, 1977 (October), 41(2), 347-353.

Elderly Crime Victims: Personal Accounts of Fears and Attacks. _Hearing before the Sub-Committee on Housing and Consumer Interests of the Select Committee on Aging, House of Representatives_ (94th Cong., 2nd Sess.) 1976.

Ferguson, E.J. _Protecting the Vulnerable Adult_. Ann Arbor, Michigan: Institute of Gerontology, Uuniversity of Michigan-Wayne State University, 1978.

Fuller, S.S. "Inhibiting Helplessness in Elderly People." _Journal of Gerontological Nursing_, 1978, 4(4), 18-21.

Goldsmith, J. and Goldsmith, S. "Overview of Crimes Against the Elderly." Statement Before Select Committee on Aging, House of Representatives (96th Cong., 2nd Sess.) 1978.

Goldsmith, J. and Thomas, N.E. "Crimes Against the Elderly." _Aging_, June/July 1974.

Horowitz, A. "Families Who Care: A Study of Natural Support Systems of the Elderly." Paper presented at 31st Annual Scientific Meeting, Gerontological Society, Dallas, Texas, 1978.

Kastenbaum, R. and Durkee, N. "Young People View Old Age." In R. Kastenbaum (Ed.) _New Thoughts on Old Age_. Springer, New York, 1964.

Lau, E. and Kosberg, J. "Abuse of the Elderly by Informal Care Providers: Practice and Research Issues." 31st Annual Meeting of the Gerontological Society, Dallas, Texas, 1978.

Lebowitz, B.D. Crimes Against the Elderly.
Statement Before the Joint Hearings of
the Subcommittee on Domestic and Inter-
national Scientific Planning, Analysis
and Cooperation, Committee on Science
and Technology, and the Subcommittee on
Housing and Consumer Interests, Select
Committee on Aging, House of Representatives
(96th Congress, 1st Session), January 31,
1978.

O'Malley, Helen. Segars, Howard, Perez, Rubin.
"Elder Abuse in Massachusetts: A Survey
of Professionals and Paraprofessionals."
Boston: Legal Research and Services for
the Elderly, 1979.

O'Malley, H. "Elder Abuse: A Review of the
Literature." Boston: Legal Research and
Services for the Elderly.

Steinmetz, S.K. and Straus, M.A. Violence in
the Family. New York: Harper & Row, 1974.

Strauss, M.A., Gelles, R.J., and Steinmetz, S.
K. Closed Doors: Violence in the American
Family. Garden City, N.Y.: Anchor Press/
Doubleday, 1980.

Victims of Family Violence Include Elderly
Relatives. Criminal Justice and the Elderly
Newsletter, Fall, 1978, 12.

Walshe-Brennan, K. "Granny Bashing." Nursing
Mirror, December 22, 1977, 32-34.

Zola, I.K. "Feelings About Age Among Older
People." Journal of Gerontology, 1962, 17
65-68.

Appendix A
STATUS OF ELDERLY ABUSE PREVENTION LEGISLATION

State	Adult protective service law?	Year passed	Mandatory reporting provisions	Legislation pending
Alabama	Yes	1977	Yes	No.
Alaska	No		No	No.
Arizona	Yes	1980	No	No.
Arkansas	Yes	1977	Yes	No.
California	No		No	Yes.
Colorado	No		No	Yes.
Connecticut	Yes	1978	Yes	No.
Delaware	No		No	Yes.
Florida	Yes	1977	Yes	No.
Georgia	No		No	Yes.
Hawaii	No		No	No.
Idaho	No		No	No.
Illinois	No		No	No.
Indiana	No		No	No.
Iowa	No		No	No.
Kansas	Yes	1980	No	No.
Kentucky	Yes	1976	Yes	No.
Louisiana	No		No	No.
Maine	Yes	1964	No	Yes.
Maryland	Yes	1977	No	No.
Massachusetts	Yes	1980	No	Yes.
Michigan	Yes	1976	No	Yes.
Minnesota	Yes	1980	Yes	Yes.
Mississippi	No		No	Yes.
Missouri	Yes	1980	Yes	Yes.
Montana	Yes	1975	No	No.
Nebraska	Yes	1978	Yes	No.
Nevada	No		No	No.
New Hampshire	Yes	1977	Yes	No.
New Jersey	No		No	Yes.
New Mexico	No		No	Yes.
New York	Yes	1979	No	Yes.
North Carolina	Yes	1973	Yes	No.
North Dakota	No		No	Yes.
Ohio	No		No	Yes.
Oklahoma	Yes	1977	Yes	No.
Oregon	No		No	Yes.
Pennsylvania	No		No	Yes.
Rhode Island	Yes	1980	No	No.
South Carolina	Yes	1974	Yes	No.
South Dakota	No		No	No.
Tennessee	Yes	1978	Yes	No.
Texas	No		No	No.
Utah	Yes	1977	Yes	No.
Vermont	Yes	1980	Yes	No.
Virginia	Yes	1977	Yes	Yes.
Washington	No		No	Yes.
West Virginia	No		No	Yes.
Wisconsin	Yes	1973	No	No.
Wyoming	No		No	Yes.
District of Columbia	No		No	Yes.
Puerto Rico	No		No	Yes.

Appendix B
MODEL ADULT PROTECTIVE
SERVICES ACT*

INTRODUCTORY COMMENTS

As with any model statute, the general purpose of the Model Protective Services Act is to provide prototype legislation which the States may utilize in drafting their own protective services statutes. This act also has three particular objectives: (1) To provide the authority for a State to develop, organize, and supervise a State program of protective services; (2) to outline guidelines and criteria for the design and operation of a protective services system; (3) to authorize the courts to issue orders for involuntary protective services and protective placement after making specific findings and following designated procedures.

The last objective should be seen in a wider context. All States currently permit certain types of involuntary intervention in the lives of their citizens, including the elderly. The kinds of intervention relevant to the elderly are typically authorized through civil commitment proceedings involving admission to a State mental hospital or guardianship proceedings transferring authority over the ward or his property to a court-appointed fiduciary. This act does not modify or replace such legislation, but rather is intended to provide legal authority to intervene involuntarily in situations requiring less drastic interference with a person's civil rights.

Two specific situations receive particular attention. The first concerns the person whose health or living conditions pose serious danger to himself or others and consequently short-term emergency action is necessary. The court order for this problem is called an "emergency order for protective services." Intervention for a longer period must follow the existing guardianship laws.

The other situation for which legally authorized intervention is necessary is the involuntary transfer of an elderly person's residence to an institution other than a mental hospital, such as a nursing home. This intervention is referred to as "protective placement."

In both instances, current State law concerning civil commitment or guardianship is either wide of the mark, which is to fill a particular need of a person, or offers too drastic a solution by declaring the person incompetent and stripping him of all or most of his rights. The Model Protective Services Act attempts to fill the gaps in existing law and at the same time to authorize only the least restrictive and appropriate form of intervention.

This explanation of the act's methods for authorizing involuntary intervention through legal channels should not, however, divert attention from the act's other objectives. The protective services system contemplated by this act will function on a voluntary basis in the

*Source: "Protective Services for the Elderly," a working paper, prepared for the Special Committee on Aging, U.S. Senate, July 1977.

vast majority of cases. Indeed, a system which requires frequent involuntary intervention may well be suspect. It is expected that the wide range of services provided in this system to assist the elderly in maintaining independent lifestyles will prove attractive to them and invite their cooperation. The potential for involuntary intervention and, hopefully, its infrequent but necessary occurrence under the provisions of this act, will distinguish the protective services system created by this act from existing programs of home or community-centered services.

Accompanying the Model Protective Services Act is other suggested legislation. One important adjunct is the Model Public Guardian Act designed to provide guardianship services for the financially needy. Suggested revisions of the State guardianship, conservatorship, and power of atttorneys laws based largely on the Uniform Probate Code are also proposed. The final proposal contains a short but significant change in State civil commitment to require courts to consider whether less drastic alternative programs than commitment are available and adequate.

The net results of the enactment of all this proposed legislation will be a program of services to the elderly to assist them to avoid institutionalization and a spectrum of alternative forms of legally authorized intervention in the elderly person's life calibrated to provide only the specific services necessary to meet immediate needs and avoid more drastic interference.

SUGGESTED LEGISLATION

(Title, enacting clause, etc.)

SECTION. 1. (Short title.) This act may be cited as the Adult Protective Services Act.

SECTION 2. (Declaration of Policy and Legislative Intent.) The legislature of the State of [————] recognizes that many elderly citizens of the State, because of the infirmities of aging, are unable to manage their own affairs or to protect themselves from exploitation, abuse, neglect, or physical danger. Often such persons cannot find others able or willing to render assistance. The legislature intends through this act to establish a system of protective services designed to fill this need and to assure their availability to all elderly citizens. It is also the intent of the legislature to authorize only the least possible restriction on the exercise of personal and civil rights consistent with the person's need for services, and to require that due process be followed in imposing such restrictions.

Comments on section 2

The protective services system established by this act is designed to benefit only the elderly because, as an identifiable segment of society, their need for such services is imperative. Moreover, many States have already developed for their elderly citizens systems of supportive and preventive services which can be readily integrated into the proposed protective services system. The additional costs of the proposed program for the elderly will therefore be small, as compared with the costs of creating an entirely new services program 'for all residents of the State.

89

Section 3. Definitions—As used in this act:

(1) "Conservator" means a person who is appointed by a court to manage the estate of a protected person.

(2) "Court" means the court or branch having jurisdiction in matters relating to the affairs of decedents, this court in this State is known as [   ].

(3) "Department" means the [State agency responsible for community-based services to the elderly].

(4) "Elderly" means a person 60 years of age or older, who is a resident of the State.

(5) "Emergency" means that an elderly person is living in conditions which present a substantial risk of death or immediate and serious physical harm to himself or others.

(6) "Emergency services" are protective services furnished to an elderly person in an emergency pursuant to the provisions of section 10 of this act.

(7) "Geriatric evaluation service" is a team of medical, psychological, psychiatric, and social work professionals established by the [State agency responsible for community-based services to the elderly] for the purpose of conducting a comprehensive physical, mental, and social evaluation of an elderly person for whom a petition has been filed in a court for commitment to a mental hospital, appointment of a conservator or guardian, an emergency order for protective services, or an order for protective placement.

(8) "Guardian" means a person who has qualified as a guardian of an incapacitated person pursuant to testamentary or court appointment, but excludes one who is merely a guardian ad litem.

(9) "Hazardous living conditions" means a mode of life which contains a substantial risk of or actual exploitation, abuse, neglect, or physical danger.

(10) "Incapacitated person" means [alternative A: any person who is impaired by reason of mental illness, mental deficiency, physical illness or disability, advanced age, chronic use of drugs, chronic intoxication, or other causes (except minority) to the extent that he lacks sufficient understanding or capacity to make or communicate responsible decisions concerning his person]. [Alternative B: any person for whom a guardian has been appointed by the court.]

(11) "Independent living arrangements" means a mode of life maintained on a continuing basis outside of a hospital, Veterans' Administration hospital, nursing home, or other facility licensed by or under the jurisdiction of any State agency.

(12) "Infirm person" means a person who, because of physical or mental disability, is substantially impaired in his ability to provide adequately for his own care or custody.

(13) "Interested person" means any adult relative or friend of an elderly person, or any official or representative of a protective services agency or of any public or nonprofit agency, corporation, board or organization eligible for designation as a protective services agency.

(14) A "protected person" is a person for whom a conservator has been appointed or other protective order has been made.

(15) "Protective placement" means the transfer of an elderly person from independent living arrangements to a hospital, nursing home, or domiciliary or residential care facility, or from one such institution to another, for a period anticipated to last longer than 6 days.

(16) "Protective services" means the services furnished by a protective service agency or its delegate, as described in section 6 of this act.

(17) "Protective services agency" means a public or nonprofit private agency, corporation, board or organization authorized by the Department pursuant to section 4(f) of this act to furnish protective services to elderly infirm, protected or incapacitated persons and/or to serve as conservators or guardians of the person for elderly protected or incapacitated persons upon appointment by a court.

(18) "Public guardian" means the office of the public guardian.

(19) A "ward" is a person for whom a guardian has been appointed.

Comments on section 3

The terminology of the Uniform Probate Code has been adopted here to describe the persons principally involved in guardianship and conservatorship proceedings. "Incapacitated persons" are those for whom guardians (of the person) are appointed, while "protected persons" are those for whom conservators have been appointed or other protective orders issued by a court.

The term "infirm persons" refers to the elderly whose degree of impairment is substantial, but is not so serious as to justify appointment of a guardian or conservator.

SECTION 4. Establishment of protective services system.

(a) Planning and development of system.—The Department shall develop a coordinated system of protective services for elderly infirm and incapacitated persons. In planning this system, the Department shall obtain the advice of agencies, corporations, boards, and associations currently involved in the provision of social, health, legal, nutritional and other services to the elderly, as well as of organizations of the elderly themselves.

(b) Advisory board.—In order to provide continuing advice to the Department concerning the protective services system, an advisory board composed of [nine] members appointed by the Governor is established.

(c) Provision of services by Department.—The Department may provide direct protective services.

(d) Contracts for services.—The Department may contract with any protective service agency for the provision of protective services.

(e) Utilization of resources.—The Department shall utilize to the extent appropriate and available existing resources and services of public and nonprofit private agencies in providing protective services.

(f) Designation of protective services agencies.—The Department may designate any public or nonprofit private agency, corporation, board or organization as a protective services agency. The Department shall issue regulations establishing criteria and procedures for the designation of protective services agencies. Preference shall be given to agencies with consumer or other citizen representation.

(*g*) Limitation.—No public or private agency, corporation, board or organization may furnish protective services to an elderly person under court order or serve as guardian of the person unless the Department has designated such a body as a protective services agency pursuant to subsection (*f*) above.

(*h*) Emergencies.—The Department shall designate at least one protective services agency in each [city and county] which shall be responsible for rendering protective services in an emergency.

(*i*) Coordination and supervision of system.—Upon establishment of the protective services system, the Department shall be responsible for continuing coordination and supervision of the system. In carrying out these duties, the Department shall:

(1) Adopt rules and regulation for the system;

(2) Continuously monitor the effectiveness of the system and perform evaluative research about it; and

(3) Utilize to the extent available grants from Federal, State, and other public and private sources to support the system.

Comments on section 4

This section sets forth the powers and duties of the State agency responsible for organizing a protective services system. The structure and detailed organization of this system, however, are left to the agency and are not included in the legislation.

The chief duties of the agency are: (1) to develop a protective services system; (2) to obtain wide ranging professional and consumer advice in planning and operating the system; (3) as part of the system, to designate local protective services agencies for emergency situations; and (4) to coordinate and supervise the system on an ongoing basis.

The State agency is given a variety of powers in providing protective services, but States may wish to select those it believes most in accord with its system and resources and therefore delete other powers. Thus the agency itself may provide protective services; it may contract for these services at State expense; it may simply designate existing organizations as providers of protective services; or it may choose a combination of these approaches. Subsection (*e*) states a preference for the use of existing community resources, while subsection (*h*) indicates a further preference for organizations with broad citizen representation.

Where protective services are to be furnished by an organization, subsection (*g*) requires this organization to be approved for this purpose by the State agency. The requirement for approval as well as its power will enable the State agency to limit the provision of services to responsible organizations which meet agency criteria.

SECTION 5. Protective services agencies.

(*a*) Powers.—A protective services agency is authorized:

(1) to furnish protective services to an elderly person with his consent;

(2) to petition the court for appointment of a conservator or guardian, for issuance of an emergency order for protective services, or for an order for protective placement;

(3) to furnish protective services to an elderly infirm person without his consent on an emergency basis pursuant to section 10 of this act;

(4) to furnish protective services to an elderly incapacitated or protected person with the consent of such person's guardian or conservator;

(5) to serve as conservator, guardian, or temporary guardian of an elderly protected or incapacitated person;

(6) to enter into protective arrangements and to conduct single transactions authorized by a court pursuant to [section 5–409 of the Uniform Probate Code].

(*b*) Reports.—A protective services agency shall make such reports as the Department or a court may require.

Comments on section 5

Once having been designated a "protective services agency" by the State agency, the protective services agency is required to obtain permission before it may provide services. This permission may come from the elderly person himself (subsection (*a*)(1)), that person's conservator or guardian (subsection (*a*)(4)), or a court. Court authorization will be given by issuance of an emergency order (subsection (*a*)(3)), by appointment of the protective services agency as conservator or guardian (subsection (*a*)(5)), or by granting power to conduct particular transactions for the elderly person (subsection (*a*)(6)).

The protective services agency is also empowered under subsection (*a*)(2) to petition the court for appointment of a conservator or guardian and for issuance of orders for protective services on an emergency basis or for protective placement.

Section 6. Nature of Protective Services.

(*a*) Definition.—Protective services are services furnished by a protective services agency or its delegate to an elderly infirm, incapacitated, or protected person with the person's consent or appropriate legal authority, in order to assist the person in performing the activities of daily living, and thereby maintain independent living arrangements and avoid hazardous living conditions.

(*b*) Services.—The services furnished in a protective services system may include but are not limited to: social case work; psychiatric and health evaluation; home care; day care; legal assistance; social services; health care; and other services consistent with the purpose of this act. Such services do not include protective placement.

(*c*) Service-related activities.—In order to provide the services listed in subsection (*a*) above, a protective services system may include but is not limited to the following service-related activities: outreach; identifying persons in need of services; counselling; referring persons for services; evaluating individuals; arranging for services; tracking and following up cases; referring persons to the public guardian; petitioning the courts for the appointment of a conservator or guardian of the person; and other activities consistent with the purposes of this act.

(*d*) Costs of services.—The costs of providing protective services shall be borne by the provider of such services, unless the elderly person agrees to pay for them or a court authorizes the provider to receive reasonable reimbursement from the person's assets after a finding that the person is financially able to make such payment.

Comments on section 6

The definition of protective services in subsection (*a*) indicates that such services are intended to be only a specific portion of a broader program whose purpose is to prevent or delay institutionalization of the elderly. The characteristics that distinguish protective services from these larger programs are: (1) their target population is the infirm, incapacitated, or protected elderly: (2) the services are provided by a designated protective services agency or its delegate; and (3) unless the elderly client consents to accept the services, the protective service agency may intervene only with court authorization.

Subsections (*b*) and (*c*) provide examples of the services that may be included in a protective services program. Protective placement, defined in section 3(15) above, is excluded from these services. Section 11 establishes special proceedings to obtain court authorization for involuntary transfers of residence.

Subsection (d) establishes the presumption that the protective services will be paid for by the provider agency, which may in turn be reimbursed from Federal or State sources if such funding is available. The provider agency may obtain reimbursement from the elderly person only if the client consents or a court authorizes such payment. The criterion to be applied by the court is deliberately framed in general terms, viz, the "financial ability" of the elderly person to afford the services. See also section 9(*c*). "Financial ability" is a variable dependent on the nature, extent, and liquidity of the person's assets; his disposable net income; the type, duration and complexity of the services required and rendered; and any other foreseeable expenses.

A rigid means test should be avoided. On the other hand, elderly persons who desire to receive protective services and can afford to pay for them are not precluded from receiving them under this section.

In the event that the elderly client will pay for protective services, the criterion for reimbursement is the reasonable cost of the services. See also section 9(*c*).

SECTION 7. Geriatric evaluation service—

(*a*) Establishment.—The Department shall establish a geriatric evaluation service for the purpose of conducting a comprehensive physical, mental, and social evaluation of an elderly person for whom a petition has been filed in a court for commitment to a mental hospital, appointment of a conservator or guardian, an emergency order for protective services, or an order for protective placement.

(*b*) Evaluation.—The evaluation of an elderly person conducted by the geriatric evaluation service should include at least the following:

(1) The name and address of the place where the person is residing and of the person or agency, if any, who is providing services at present;

(2) A description of the treatment and services, if any, presently being provided to the person;

(3) An evaluation of the person's present physical, mental, and social conditions; and

(4) A recommendation concerning the least restrictive course of services, care or treatment consistent with the person's needs.

(*c*) Costs.—The cost of this evaluation should be borne by the Department.

Comments on section 7

The geriatric evaluation service (GES) is a team of medical, psychological, psychiatric, and social work professionals. Its function is to provide the courts with impartial professional advice to assist them in making determinations which by their very nature involve the assessment of an elderly person's capacity to continue independent living and decisionmaking. The direct responsibility of the GES is to the court, not the petitioner or the elderly person, and therefore its recommendations will hopefully be free of partisanship. For the same reason, the costs of this evaluation are borne by the State under subsection (*c*) instead of by the parties to the proceedings. At the same time, however, the evaluation conducted by the GES is not exclusive, and therefore the parties to the proceedings may also offer similar evaluations in evidence. See section 12(*a*) (4).

One important feature of the evaluation described in subsection (*b*)(4) is the GES' recommendation concerning the least restrictive course of services, care or treatment consistent with the elderly person's needs. The theme that intervention should be as minimal as necessary to achieve valid goals for the person appears elsewhere in the act. See sections 9(*b*), 11(*a*)(6), 11(*g*)(3), and 11(*l*). Section 14 also authorizes the elderly person to appeal the court s finding on this issue required in section 11(*a*)(6).

SECTION 8. Voluntary protective services.

(*a*) Consent required.—Any elderly person may receive protective services, provided the person requests or affirmatively consents to receive these services. If the person withdraws or refuses consent, the services shall not be provided.

(*b*) Interference with services.—No person shall interfere with the provision of protective services to an elderly person who requests or consents to receive such services. In the event that interference occurs on a continuing basis, the Department, a protective services agency, or the public guardian may petition the court to enjoin such interference.

(*c*) Publicity for services.—The Department shall publicize throughout the State the availability of protective services on a voluntary basis for elderly persons.

Comments on section 8

It is expected that protective services will ordinarily be provided to the elderly who desire such assistance. In such case, proceedings to establish guardianships or conservatorships, if necessary, will be nonadversarial.

Subsections (*b*) and (*c*) are consistent with the principle of voluntary acceptance of services by prohibiting interference with these services by others and by requiring the State agency to make the elderly aware of the availability of this assistance.

SECTION 9. Involuntary Protective Services.

(*a*) Lack of consent.—If an elderly person lacks the capacity to consent to receive protective services, these services may be ordered by a court on an involuntary basis, (1) through an emergency order pursuant to section 10 of this act, or (2) through appointment of a conservator or guardian pursuant to [the provisions of the Model Guardianship and Conservatorship Act].

(*b*) Least restrictive alternative.—In ordering involuntary protective services, the court shall authorize only that intervention which it finds to be least restrictive of the elderly person's liberty and rights, while consistent with his welfare and safety. The basis for such finding shall be stated in the record by the court.

(*c*) Payment for services.—The elderly infirm, incapacitated, or protected person shall not be required to pay for involuntary protective services unless such payment is authorized by the court upon a showing that the person is financially able to pay. In this event the court shall provide for reimbursement of the reasonable costs of the services.

Comments on section 9

Protective services may be provided to elderly persons without their consent only with court authorization. Such authorization may take two forms: (1) the issuance of an emergency order under section 10 or (2) the appointment of a conservator or guardian. If this authorization has not been obtained or has been denied and the elderly person refuses to accept the services voluntarily, no organization or individual may intervene on its own authority.

The underlying principle here is that the elderly person alone should decide whether or not to accept these services, regardless of the opinion of others about the possible detrimental effects on the person who refuses to accept assistance. Involuntary intervention authorized by the courts, therefore, requires findings that: (1) The elderly person lacks capacity to consent to services, for example, to make intelligent decisions about his person or property; and (2) that conditions exist justifying an emergency order under section 10 or appointment of a conservator or guardian. It is not enough that the older person refuses services or other persons disagree with his decisions.

Discussions of subsection (*b*) appear in the comments on section 7 and of subsection (*c*) in the comments on section 6.

SECTION 10. Emergency order for protective services.

(*a*) Petition and findings.—Upon petition by the Department, the public guardian, a protective services agency, or an interested person, a court may issue an order authorizing the provision of protective services on an emergency basis to an elderly person after finding on the record, based on clear and convincing evidence, that:

(1) the elderly person is infirm or incapacitated, as defined in section 3 of this act;

(2) an emergency exists, as defined in section 3(5) of this act;

(3) the elderly person lacks the capacity to consent to receive protective services;

(4) no person authorized by law or court order to give consent for the elderly person is available to consent to emergency services; and

(5) the proposed order is substantially supported by the findings of the geriatric evaluation service, or if not so supported, there are compelling reasons for ordering services.

(*b*) Limitations on emergency order. In issuing an emergency order, the court shall adhere to the following limitations:

(1) Only such protective services as are necessary to remove the conditions creating the emergency shall be ordered; and the court shall specifically designate the approved services in its order.

(2) Protective services authorized by an emergency order shall not include hospitalization or a change of residence unless the court specifically finds such action is necessary and gives specific approval for such action in its order.

(3) Protective services may be provided through an emergency order only for 72 hours. The original order may be renewed once for a 72 hour period upon a showing to the court that continuation of the original order is necessary to remove the emergency.

(4) In its order the court shall appoint the petitioner, another interested person, or the public guardian as temporary guardian of the elderly person with responsibility for the person's welfare and authority to give consent for the person for the approved protective services until the expiration of the order.

(5) The issuance of an emergency order and the appointment of a temporary guardian shall not deprive the elderly person of any rights except to the extent validly provided for in the order or appointment.

(6) To implement an emergency order, the court may authorize forcible entry of the premises of the elderly person for the purpose of rendering protective services or transporting the person to another location for the provision of such services only after a showing to the court that attempts to gain voluntary access to the premises have failed and forcible entry is necessary. Persons making authorized forcible entry shall be accompanied by a peace officer.

(c) Contents of petition.—The petition for an emergency order shall set forth the name, address, and interest of the petitioner; the name, age and address of the elderly person in need of protective services; the nature of the emergency; the nature of the person's disability, if determinable; the proposed protective services; the petitioner's reasonable belief, together with facts supportive thereof, as to the existence of the facts stated in subsection (a)(1) through (4) above; and facts showing petitioner's attempts to obtain the elderly person's consent to the services and the outcomes of such attempts.

(d) Notice of petition.—Notice of the filing of such petition, and other relevant information, including the factual basis of the belief that emergency services are needed and a description of the exact services to be rendered, the rights of the person in the court proceeding, and the consequences of a court order, shall be given to the person, to his spouse, or if none, to his adult children or next of kin, to his guardian, if any, to the public guardian, and to the geriatric evaluation service. Such notice shall be given in language reasonably understandable by its intended recipients at least 24 hours prior to the hearing for emergency intervention. The court may waive the 24-hour notice requirement upon showing that (1) immediate and reasonably foreseeable physical harm to the person or others will result from the 24-hour delay, and (2) reasonable attempts have been made to notify the elderly person, his spouse, or if none, his adult children or next of kin, his guardian, if any, and the public guardian. Notice of the court's final order shall also be given to the above named parties.

(*e*) Hearing on petition.—Upon receipt of a petition for an emergency order for protective services, the court shall hold a hearing pursuant to the provisions of section 12 of this act. This hearing shall be held no earlier than 24 hours after the notice required in subsection (*d*) above has been given, unless such notice has been waived by the court.

(*f*) Review of court order.—The elderly person, the temporary guardian or any interested person may petition the court to have the emergency order set aside or modified at any time, notwithstanding any prior findings by the court that the elderly person is infirm.

(*g*) Report.—Where protective services are rendered on the basis of an emergency order, the temporary guardian shall submit a report describing the circumstances including the name, place, date, and nature of the services, and the use of forcible entry, if any, to the court and the public guardian. This report shall become part of the court record.

(*h*) Continued need for services.—If the person continues to need protective services after the renewal order provided in subsection (*b*)(3) above has expired, the temporary guardian or the public guardian shall immediately petition the court to appoint a conservator or guardian and/or to order protective placement pursuant to section 11 of this act.

(*i*) Immunity of petitioner.—The petitioner shall not be liable for filing the petition if he acted in good faith.

(*j*) Emergency placement.—When from personal observation of a peace officer, it appears probable that an elderly person will suffer immediate and irreparable physical injury or death if not immediately placed in a health care facility, that the elderly person is incapable of giving consent, and that it is not possible to follow the procedures of this section, the peace officer making such observation may transport the elderly person to an appropriate medical facility. The Department and the persons entitled to notice under subsection (*d*) above shall be notified of such detention within 4 hours. The Department shall file a petition pursuant to subsection (*a*) above within 24 hours after the transfer of the elderly person has taken place. The court shall hold a hearing on this petition and render its decision within 48 hours after the transfer has occurred.

Comments on section 10

This section provides the legal authority to deal with a situation where an elderly person is living in highly dangerous conditions or is himself in a state of severe physical deterioration, and therefore swift action is necessary to provide a remedy. Despite the emergency character of the situation, court authorization on an expedited basis is still required for involuntary intervention. The only exception to the need for a court order is the provision for emergency placement in subsection (*j*).

Subsection (*a*) lists the findings which the court must make to support issuance of an order for protective services to be furnished in an emergency. These findings must be supported by "clear and convincing evidence" and not merely a preponderance of the evidence to emphasize the caution with which involuntary intervention must be authorized. The basis for these findings should appear in the court record and are appealable under section 14.

Even though a court finds issuance of an order to be justified, the scope and duration of the order are subject to the limitations of subsection (b). In conformity with the "least restrictive action" principle enunciated earlier, the court may authorize only those services needed to remove the emergency, not an extended care program of rehabilitation or treatment designed to restore the elderly person to his full potential. These services must be specified in the court order, and may not include hospitalization or a change of residence except as provided in subsection (b)(2). Two 72-hour programs of services are permissible under subsection (b)(3). If emergency protective services are needed beyond this 6-day period, proceedings for appointment of a guardian or conservator or full protective placement must be initiated, as provided in subsection (h). Forcible entry of the elderly person's premises to implement the court order is also controlled in subsection (b)(16).

To avoid having the elderly person exclusively in the care of the provider of services for the duration of the court order, subsection (b)(4) requires the court to appoint a temporary guardian for this period whose duties are to be responsible for the elderly person's welfare, and to petition for further court actions under subsection (h) if services continue to be necessary. The provider of services may be appointed as temporary guardian if the court so chooses, but it is preferable that some other party serve as guardian to prevent the elderly person from becoming completely dependent on the provider even for the limited duration of the emergency order.

This section is intended to replace for elderly persons section 5–310 of the Uniform Probate Code, which authorizes the appointment of a temporary guardian in two situations. The UPC provides that, when an incapacitated person has no guardian and an emergency exists, the court may exercise the power of a guardian pending notice and hearing. This provision appears to be unnecessary in the light of section 10 of the Adult Protective Services Act. Under the UPC a temporary guardian may also be appointed, with or without notice, when an appointed guardian is not effectively performing his duties and the court finds that the welfare of the incapacitated person requires immediate action. Again, the combination of a short-term guardianship under section 10 of this act and further proceedings for a new appointment of a permanent guardian seems better suited to protect the interests of the elderly person because of their strict criteria and procedural requirements.

Subsections (c), (d), and (e) describe the procedure to be followed by the petitioner and the court for issuance of an emergency order for protective services. A philosophy of full disclosure has been adopted, both as to the contents of the petition and as to the persons entitled to be notified of the filing of the petition. Such disclosure will afford interested parties the opportunity to intervene or participate in the proceedings, to assist the court, and to protect the interests of the elderly person.

The provision for emergency placement in subsection (j) attempts to deal with the situation where there is not sufficient time to obtain an emergency court order. Peace officers are authorized to make on-the-spot determinations based on personal observation that certain specified conditions probably exist. This determination is analogous to decisions based on probable cause, with which police are familiar in the areas of warrantless arrests and searches in criminal contexts. Once the transfer to a health care facility has occurred, however, appropriate parties must be notified of this action and regular proceedings under section 10 must be started. The court is required to reach a decision within a specified time limit because transfer of the elderly person has already occurred and should be validated or not as quickly as possible.

SECTION 11. Protective placement.

(a) Findings.—If the elderly person refuses to consent, protective placement shall not take place unless ordered by a court after a finding on the record based on clear and convincing evidence that:

(1) The elderly person is incapacitated, as defined in section 3(10) of this act [or as defined in sections ——— or ——— of the State code], and a petition to appoint a guardian accompanies this petition for protective placement;

(2) The elderly person is so totally incapable of providing for his own care or custody that his condition creates a substantial risk of serious physical harm to himself or others. Serious harm may be occasioned by overt acts or acts of omission;

(3) The elderly person has a disability which is permanent or likely to be permanent;

(4) The elderly person needs full-time residential care or treatment;

(5) The proposed order is substantially supported by the recommendation of the geriatric evaluation service, as provided for in subsection (g) below, or if not so supported, there are compelling reasons for ordering such placement; and

(6) No less restrictive alternative course of care or treatment is available which is consistent with the incapacitated person's welfare and safety.

(b) Who may petition.—The Department, a protective services agency, a conservator, a guardian, the public guardian, or a person applying for a conservatorship or guardianship pursuant to [the provisions of the uniform probate code] may petition the court for protective placement.

(c) Contents of petition.—The petition shall state with particularity the factual basis for the allegations specified in subsection (a) above and shall be based on the petitioner's personal knowledge of the elderly person alleged to need protective placement.

(d) Order of consideration.—A petition for appointment of a conservator or guardian accompanying a petition for protective placement shall be heard and decided prior to the petition for protective placement.

(e) Notice of petition.—Notice of a petition for protective placement shall be served upon the elderly person sought to be placed by personal service at least 10 days prior to the time set for a hearing. Notice shall be given in language reasonably understandable by the elderly person, and he shall be informed orally of its complete contents. The notice shall include the names of all petitioners, the factual basis of the belief that protective placement is needed, the rights of the elderly person in the court proceedings, the name and address of the proposed placement, and the consequences of an order for protective placement. The person serving the notice shall certify to the court that the petition has been delivered and notice given. Notice shall also be given to the person's guardian ad litem; legal counsel; persons having physical custody of the elderly person whose names and addresses are known to the petitioner or can with reasonable diligence be ascertained; any governmental or private body or group from whom the elderly person is known to be receiving aid; the geriatric evaluation service; the public guardian; and such other persons or entities as the court may require.

(f) Hearing on petition.—Upon receipt of a petition for protective placement, the court shall hold a hearing pursuant to the provisions of section 12 of this act.

(g) Evaluation of person.—In order to make the finding required in subsections (a) (2), (3), (4), and (6) above, the court shall direct that a comprehensive evaluation of the elderly person alleged to be in need of placement be conducted by the geriatric evaluation service. The evaluation shall include at least the following information:

> (1) The address of the place where the person is residing and the person or agency, if any, which is providing care treatment or services at present;

> (2) A résumé of the professional treatment and services provided to the person by the Department or agency, if any, in connection with the problem creating the need for placement;

> (3) A medical, psychological, a psychiatric, and social evaluation and review, where necessary, and any recommendations for or against maintenance or partial legal rights as provided in ——————— of this code. Such evaluation and review shall include recommendations for placement consistent with the least restrictive environment required.

(h) Choice of facilities.—In ordering protective placement, the court shall give consideration to the choice of residence of the elderly person. The court may order placement in such facilities as hospitals, nursing homes, domiciliary or personal care facilities, sheltered care residences, foster care homes, or other appropriate facilities. It may not order placement in facilities for the acutely mentally ill; placement in such facilities is governed by [the civil commitment provisions] of this code.

(i) Duration of order.—The court may authorize protective placement of an elderly person for a period not to exceed 6 months.

(j) Renewal of order.—At the time of the expiration of an order for protective placement, the guardian, the original petitioner, or any interested person may petition the court to extend its order for protective placement for an additional period not to exceed 6 months. The contents of the petition shall conform to the provisions of subsections (a) and (c) above. Notice of the petition for the extension of placement shall be made in conformity with subsection (e) above. The court shall hold a hearing to determine whether to renew the order. Any person entitled to a notice under subsection (e) above may appear at the hearing and challenge the petition; in this event, the court shall conduct the hearing pursuant to the provisions in section 12 of this act.

(k) Transfer.—The residence of an elderly person which has been established pursuant to an order for protective placement shall not be changed unless the court authorizes the transfer of residence after finding compelling reasons to justify the transfer.

(*l*) Temporary placement.—When an elderly person lives with his guardian, the guardian may petition the court to order an alternative temporary placement of the elderly person for good cause, such as to allow the guardian to take a vacation or to release the guardian temporarily for a family emergency. Such placement may be made for not more than 18 days, but the court may grant upon application an additional period not to exceed 30 days. The petition shall include such information as the court deems necessary and adequate. In ordering the alternative placement, the court shall provide for the least restrictive placement consistent with the needs of the elderly person and comparable to his previous residence. Petitions for alternative temporary placement shall not be granted more than once a year except in an emergency.

(*m*) Discharge from placement.—Prior to discharge from protective placement, the Geriatric Evaluation Service shall review the need for continued protective services after discharge, including the necessity for a conservator or guardian. Such recommendation and report shall be made to the Department, the public guardian, the elderly person's conservator or guardian, all persons notified of the original petition for protective placement, and the court where appropriate.

(*n*) Duties of the guardian.—A guardian of an elderly person placed under this section shall have the duty to take reasonable steps to assure that the elderly person is well treated, properly cared for, and provided with the opportunity to exercise his legal rights.

(*o*) Confidentiality of records.—Any records of the Department or other agency pertaining to an elderly person who is protected under this act or for whom an application has ever been made for such protection are not open to public inspection. Information contained in such records may not be disclosed publicly in such a manner as to identify individuals, but the record shall be available upon application for cause to persons approved by the court.

(*p*) Voluntary request for placement.—Any elderly person may request protective placement under this act. No legal rights are relinquished or modified as a result of such placement.

(*q*) Costs of placement.—The costs of providing protective placement shall be borne by the elderly person, unless he is placed in a public facility or is eligible for assistance under Federal or State programs, or the facility is willing to provide placement without charge.

Comments on section 11

An involuntary change of residence of an elderly person to an institutional setting, or from one institution to another, often produces major effects in the person's physical and mental health as well as in his civil rights, and therefore special proceedings to authorize such actions are necessary. The degree of incapacity required to justify protective placement as compared with protective services is greater, in that for the former the person must be found to be incapacitated to the extent that appointment of a guardian is justified. The definition of an "incapacitated person" in subsection (*a*)(1) is presented in the alternative to permit a jurisdiction with a different definition in its guardianship laws to utilize that definition in lieu of the one offered in section 3(10) of this act. The other findings required in subsection (a), particularly as to the gravity of the person's disability and its consequent risk of harm to others or himself, again emphasize that orders for protective placement should be given only when a solid justification for such action has been established in court.

The procedural provisions of subsections (c), (e), and (j) generally follow those discussed earlier under section 10 for emergency orders for protective services. Because the order for protective placement requires a finding that the person is incapacitated, subsection (d) requires that the accompanying petition for appointment of a guardian be heard and decided first, in that such appointment includes a finding of incapacity.

The role of the geriatric evaluation service has already been discussed under section 7.

Subsection (h) requires the court to consider the preference of the elderly person himself for placement, even though by definition he has refused consent to such action. This section may not be used as a vehicle to avoid the State's civil commitment law, and therefore the court may not authorize placement in a mental hospital.

Orders for protective placement are only temporary; that is, 6 months in duration, under subsection (i). The burden to obtain renewal of the order is placed by subsection (j) on a party other than the elderly person. If no such party seeks renewal, the elderly person is free to leave the residence established by the last court order. To obtain renewal of the order, the petitioner must file a petition similar in form to that previously filed and notify the persons previously entitled to notice. The court's hearing on the petition for renewal, however, may be of an ex-parte nature unless the elderly person himself or any other party entitled to notice desires to contest the petition. In this event, a hearing pursuant to section 12 must be held.

Subsection (k) places an additional burden of justification on a petitioner who wishes to transfer again the residence of a person who has already experienced displacement as a result of an order for protective placement. This provision is designed to prevent transfers of "convenience" intended to benefit the provider or the petitioner rather than the elderly person.

Subsection (m) requires the geriatric evaluation service to evaluate the person's need for assistance if discharge from protective placement occurs. The GES' recommendations are intended to assist the guardian or conservator in caring for the person or his property. If the guardianship or conservatorship is also terminated upon discharge, then the elderly person is free to accept or not the GES' recommendations.

Subsection (n) emphasizes that a guardian of an institutionalized person has a special responsibility to monitor the care and treatment of this person. If this care and treatment prove deficient, the guardian should exercise the remedies provided by Federal or State law.

Unlike section 6(d) which placed initial responsibility for the costs of protective services on the provider, subsection (g) makes the elderly person himself primarily responsible for the costs of protective placement. This principle is consistent with current Federal and State law concerning institutional care of the elderly. The alternative of making the institution responsible without providing for reimbursement would create insurmountable difficulties and nullify protective placement except for those eligible for governmental assistance.

SECTION 12. Hearing on petition.

(a) Hearing procedure.—The hearing on a petition for an emergency order for protective services or for an order for protective placement shall be held under the following conditions:

(1) The elderly person shall be present unless he has knowingly and voluntarily waived the right to be present or cannot be present because of physical or mental incapacity. Waiver or incapacity may not be presumed from nonappearance but shall be determined on the basis of factual information supplied to the court by counsel or a visitor appointed by the court.

(2) The elderly person has the right to counsel whether or not he is present at the hearing, unless he intelligently and voluntarily waives the right. If the person is indigent or lacks the capacity to waive counsel, the court shall appoint counsel. Where the person is indigent, the State shall pay reasonable attorney's fees; that is, such compensation as is customarily charged by attorneys in this State for comparable services.

(3) The elderly person shall have the right to trial by jury upon request by the person or his counsel.

(4) The elderly person has the right at his own expense, or if indigent at the expense of the State, to secure an independent medical and/or psychological or psychiatric examination relevant to the issue involved in any hearing under this section, and to present a report of this independent evaluation or the evaluator's personal testimony as evidence at the hearing.

(5) The elderly person may present evidence and cross-examine witnesses.

(b) Duties of counsel.—The duties of counsel representing an elderly person for whom a petition for an emergency order for protective services or for an order of protective placement has been filed shall include: personally interviewing the elderly person; counselling the person with respect to this act, his rights, and any available alternative resources or causes of action; arranging for an independent medical and/or psychological or psychiatric examination of the person relevant to the issue involved in the hearing; and providing competent representation at all proceedings.

(c) Statement of findings.—The court shall issue for the record a statement of its findings in support of any order for emergency protective services or protective placement.

Comments on section 12

Subsection (a) sets forth the basic procedural rights of the elderly person at hearings on petitions for an emergency order for protective services or an order for protective placement. In some details these provisions are more protective of the person than many State laws concerning guardianship and conservatorship, or even the Uniform Probate Code itself. This added protection appears warranted by the

104

substantial deprivation of personal liberty which may be the outcome of these hearings.

If anything, those States should consider strengthening the procedural rights of parties who are the subject of guardianship and conservatorship proceedings to emphasize the fact that such proceedings are at root adversarial in nature, and rightly so, and therefore the paternalistic undercurrents of many older laws should be abandoned. The rights and interests of all parties to these proceedings are best preserved when proceedings are truly adversarial.

The right to counsel provided in subsection (a)(2) is of special importance in these proceedings. Waiver of the right is permitted, but the court should exercise caution in concluding that the person is waiving this right, because the petitions in these cases may be based on allegations of mental incapacity of the person to make responsible decisions. If these allegations are taken at face value, then a waiver of the right to counsel may be subject to the same incapacity.

This subsection and subsection (a)(4) require the State to afford the indigent elderly counsel and professional evaluations at public expense. Counsel might be provided through legal aid or legal services offices or by the Public Defender. In appointing counsel the courts should be sensitive to their responsibility to appoint as counsel, where possible, attorneys with special competence or expertise in mental health proceedings.

Subsection (b), by listing in detail some of the duties of counsel, is intended to avoid permitting attorneys to provide only pro forma representation similar to that given by the guardian ad litem in many jurisdictions.

SECTION 13. Duty to report.

(a) Nature of duty.—Any person having reasonable cause to believe that an elderly person is infirm, incapacitated, or in need of protection shall report such information to the Department or the public guardian.

(b) Procedure for reporting.—The report may be made orally or in writing. It shall include the name, age, and address of the elderly person; the name and address of any other person responsible for the elderly person's care; the nature and extent of the elderly person's condition; the basis of the reporter's knowledge; and other relevant information.

(c) Immunity.—Any person making a report pursuant to subsection (a) above, testifying in any judicial proceeding arising from the report, or participating in a required evaluation, shall be immune from civil or criminal liability on account of such report, testimony, or participation, unless such person acted in bad faith or with a malicious purpose.

(d) Action on report.—Upon receipt of a report, the Department shall make a prompt and thorough evaluation to determine whether the elderly person is in need of protective services and what services are needed, unless the Department determines that the report is frivolous or is patently without a factual basis. The evaluation shall include a visit to the person and consultation with others having knowledge of the facts of the particular case. After completing the evaluation, the director shall make a written report of his findings to the elderly person, his spouse or next of kin, and the person making the report.

If the director determines that the elderly person needs protective services according to the criteria set forth in section 10(*a*) of this act, the director, the elderly person, his spouse or any interested person may petition the court for an emergency order for protective services pursuant to section 10 of this act.

Comments on section 13

Subsection (*a*) imposes a duty on all citizens to inform the State agency or the public guardian of the status of persons who are believed to be infirm, incapacitated, or in need of protection. No penalty, however, is imposed on one who fails to make such a report. Subsection (*c*) authorizes immunity from civil or criminal liability for persons making a report, except where the reporter acted in bad faith or with a malicious purpose, such as intent to harass the elderly person or to force the person to undertake a transaction against his will. The State agency is expected to investigate all such reports unless it finds that the report is frivolous or clearly without a basis in fact.

SECTION 14. Right to appeal.

An elderly person, his conservator or guardian may appeal any findings of a court under sections 10(*a*), 11(*a*), 11(*j*), or 11(*k*) of this act. Such appeal shall be handled on an expedited basis by the appellate court.

Comments on section 14

The provision for an explicit right to appeal particular findings of a court is consistent with the act's philosophy that the proceedings authorized under it be truly adversarial and that the findings of courts be specific and based on clear evidence.

SECTION 15. Severability. (Insert severability clause.)

SECTION 16. Repeal. (Insert repealer clause.)

SECTION 17. Effective date. (Insert effective date.)

○

Appendix C
SURVEY RESULTS OF THE NATIONAL COMMISSION ON THE CAUSES AND PREVENTION OF VIOLENCE 10/68

Childhood Violence	Race		Sex		Region				Income			Education				Age			
	White	Black	Male	Female	East	Midwest	South	West	$5,000 or less	$5,000 to $9,999	$10,000 or more	8th grade or less	Some high school	High school graduate	College	30 and under	31 through 50	51 through 65	65+
Percent who:																			
Were spanked as children:																			
Frequently	43	30	33	31	27	26	42	33	38	35	23	42	41	29	22	32	29	38	34
Sometimes	54	53	62	61	65	65	53	63	54	61	69	49	54	65	71	64	67	53	53
Have ever spanked a child:	84	84	78	90	79	85	88	84	81	85	87	82	86	89	80	79	94	81	73
Agree that "What young people need most of all is strong discipline by their parents":	88	86	84	89	82	87	91	85	87	89	82	90	92	89	77	81	87	88	92
Could approve of a public schoolteacher's hitting a student:	55	49	53	46	46	52	50	51	48	47	54	50	46	48	53	44	53	48	48
Could approve of a parent's beating his or her child:	23	6	11	7	17	4	8	4	8	9	8	10	11	8	7	12	7	9	5
Agree that "When a boy is growing up, it is very important for him to have a few fistfights":	75	69	68	71	69	74	65	73	72	72	65	70	77	73	62	71	66	66	72

Source: R. Stark and J. McEvoy, III. Middle Class Violence, Psychology Today, 1970, 4, p.54.

Adult Violence	Race		Sex		Region				Income			Education				Age			
	White	Black	Male	Female	East	Midwest	South	West	$5,000 or less	$5,000 to $9,999	$10,000 or more	8th grade or less	Some high school	High school graduate	College	30 and under	31 through 50	51 through 65	65+
Percent who:																			
1) Have been slapped or kicked by another person:	18	13	13	12	15	15	9	17	12	16	14	11	15	12	17	16	14	15	6
2) Have been slapped or kicked another person:	22	18	22	13	17	19	14	23	14	19	20	15	20	16	20	18	21	17	10
3) Have been punched or beaten by another person:	17	12	19	4	16	10	8	9	11	13	13	14	9	13	12	10	15	10	5
4) Have been punched or beaten another person:	20	13	21	4	15	12	7	20	7	16	15	9	19	11	13	15	14	10	4
5) Could approve of a husband's slapping his wife's face:	25	20	25	16	22	18	16	26	14	22	23	16	23	17	25	26	23	15	11
6) Could approve of a wife's slapping her husband's face:	27	22	26	19	24	21	18	25	18	24	24	19	22	18	28	33	20	18	13
7) Have been threatened with, or actually cut with a knife:	11	8	12	3	8	5	10	11	9	8	8	7	10	6	9	11	7	7	7
8) Have been threatened with a gun or shot at:	9	6	10	2	6	4	7	9	6	7	7	9	6	7	5	9	5	8	4
9) Have had to defend themselves with a knife or gun:	14	4	10	2	10	3	5	5	5	5	8	4	7	5	6	9	6	4	2
10) Own firearms:	27	43	50	32	24	45	50	46	34	41	47	40	39	41	43	38	47	40	36

108

97TH CONGRESS
1ST SESSION

H. R. 769

To provide financial assistance for programs for the prevention, identification, and treatment of elder abuse, neglect, and exploitation, to establish a National Center on Elder Abuse, and for other purposes.

IN THE HOUSE OF REPRESENTATIVES

JANUARY 6, 1981

Ms. OAKAR (for herself and Mr. PEPPER) introduced the following bill; which was referred jointly to the Committees on Education and Labor and Energy and Commerce

---

A BILL

To provide financial assistance for programs for the prevention, identification, and treatment of elder abuse, neglect, and exploitation, to establish a National Center on Elder Abuse, and for other purposes.

1   *Be it enacted by the Senate and House of Representa-*
2 *tives of the United States of America in Congress assembled,*

3   SHORT TITLE

4   SECTION 1. This Act may be cited as the "Prevention,
5 Identification, and Treatment of Elder Abuse Act of 1981".

109

SEC. 2. (a) The Secretary of Health and Human Services (hereinafter referred to in this Act as "Secretary") shall establish an office to be known as the National Center on Elder Abuse (hereinafter referred to in this Act as the "Center").

(b) The Secretary, through the Center, shall—

(1) compile, publish, and disseminate a summary annually of recently conducted research on elder abuse, neglect, and exploitation;

(2) develop and maintain an information clearinghouse on all programs, including private programs, showing promise of success, for the prevention, identification, and treatment of elder abuse, neglect, and exploitation;

(3) compile, publish, and disseminate training materials for personnel who are engaged or intend to engage in the prevention, identification, and treatment of elder abuse, neglect, and exploitation;

(4) provide technical assistance (directly or through grant or contract) to public and nonprofit private agencies and organizations to assist them in planning, improving, developing, and carrying out programs and activities relating to the special problems of elder abuse, neglect, and exploitation;

SEC. 3. For purposes of this Act—

(1) the term "abuse" means the willful infliction of injury, unreasonable confinement, intimidation, or cruel punishment with resulting physical harm or pain or mental anguish; or the willful deprivation by a caretaker of goods or services which are necessary to avoid physical harm, mental anguish, or mental illness;

(2) the term "elder" means any person who has attained the age of sixty years;

(3) the term "caretaker" means an individual who has the responsibility for the care of an elder, either voluntarily, by contract, receipt of payment for care as a result of family relationship, or by order of a court of competent jurisdiction;

(4) the term "exploitation" means the illegal or improper act or process of a caretaker using the resources of an elder for monetary or personal benefit, profit, or gain;

(5) the term "neglect" means the failure to provide for oneself the goods or services which are necessary to avoid physical harm, mental anguish or mental illness or the failure of a caretaker to provide such goods or services; and

1   (5) conduct research into the causes of elder
2   abuse, neglect, and exploitation, and into the preven-
3   tion, identification, and treatment thereof; and

4   (6) make a complete study and investigation of
5   the national incidence of elder abuse, neglect, and ex-
6   ploitation, including a determination of the extent to
7   which incidents of elder abuse, neglect, and exploita-
8   tion are increasing in number or severity.

9 The Secretary shall establish research priorities for making
10 grants or contracts under paragraph (5) of this subsection
11 and, not less than sixty days before establishing such prior-
12 ities, shall publish in the Federal Register for public comment
13 a statement of such proposed priorities.

14   (c) The Secretary may carry out functions under subsec-
15 tion (b) of this section either directly or by way of grant or
16 contract. The Secretary shall promulgate regulations setting
17 forth criteria for programs receiving funding under this sub-
18 section and shall review programs funded under this subsec-
19 tion to determine whether such programs comply with such
20 criteria. The Secretary shall, within thirty days after any de-
21 termination by the Secretary that a program fails to comply
22 with such criteria, terminate funding for such program.

23   (d) The Secretary shall make available to the Center
24 such staff and resources as are necessary for the Center to
25 carry out effectively its functions under this Act.

1   (6) the term "physical harm" means bodily pain,
2   injury, impairment, or disease.

3   DEMONSTRATION PROGRAMS AND PROJECTS

4   SEC. 4. (a) The Secretary, through the Center, is au-
5   thorized to make grants to, and enter into contracts with,
6   public agencies or nonprofit organizations (or combinations
7   thereof) for demonstration programs and projects designed to
8   prevent, identify, and treat elder abuse, neglect, and exploita-
9   tion. Grants or contracts under this subsection may be—

10   (1) for the development and establishment of
11   training programs for professional and paraprofessional
12   personnel, in the fields of health, law, gerontology,
13   social work, and other relevant fields, who are engaged
14   in, or intend to work in. the field of prevention, identi-
15   fication, and treatment of elder abuse, neglect, and
16   exploitation;

17   (2) for the establishment and maintenance of cen-
18   ters, serving defined geographic areas, staffed by multi-
19   disciplinary teams of personnel trained in the special
20   problems of elder abuse, neglect, and exploitation
21   cases, to provide a broad range of services related to
22   elder abuse, neglect, and exploitation, including direct
23   support and supervision of sheltered housing programs,
24   as well as providing advice and consultation to individ-

113

1 uals, agencies, and organizations which request such

2 services; and

3 (3) for furnishing services of teams of professional

4 and paraprofessional personnel who are trained in the

5 special problems of elder abuse, neglect, and exploita-

6 tion cases, on a consulting basis, to small communities

7 where such services are not available.

8 (b)(1) The Secretary, through the Center, is authorized

9 to make grants to the States for the purpose of assisting the

10 States in developing, strengthening, and carrying out elder

11 abuse, neglect, and exploitation prevention and treatment

12 programs.

13 (2) In order for a State to qualify for assistance under

14 this subsection, such State shall—

15 (A) have in effect a State elder abuse, neglect,

16 and exploitation law which shall include provisions for

17 immunity for persons reporting instances of elder

18 abuse, neglect, and exploitation, from prosecution aris-

19 ing out of such reporting, under any State or local law;

20 (B) provide for the mandatory reporting of known

21 and suspected instances of elder abuse, neglect, and

22 exploitation;

23 (C) provide that upon receipt of a report of known

24 or suspected instances of elder abuse, neglect, or ex-

25 ploitation an investigation shall be initiated promptly to

1   substantiate the accuracy of the report, and, upon a
2   finding of abuse, neglect, or exploitation, steps shall be
3   taken to protect the health and welfare of the abused,
4   neglected, or exploited elder;

5   (D) demonstrate that there are in effect through-
6   out the State in connection with the enforcement of
7   elder abuse, neglect, and exploitation laws and with
8   the reporting of suspected instances of elder abuse, ne-
9   glect, and exploitation, such administrative procedures,
10   such personnel trained in the special problems of elder
11   abuse, neglect, and exploitation prevention and treat-
12   ment, such training procedures, such institutional and
13   other facilities (public and private), and such related
14   multidisciplinary programs and services as may be nec-
15   essary or appropriate to assure that the State will deal
16   effectively with elder abuse, neglect, and exploitation
17   cases in the State;

18   (E) provide for methods to preserve the confiden-
19   tiality of records in order to protect the rights of the
20   elder;

21   (F) provide for the cooperation of law enforcement
22   officials, courts of competent jurisdiction, and State
23   agencies providing human services with respect to spe-
24   cial problems of elder abuse, neglect, and exploitation;

1   (G) provide that the elder participate in decisions
2   regarding his or her own welfare, and provide that the
3   least restrictive alternatives are available to the elder
4   who is abused, neglected, or exploited;

5   (H) provide that the aggregate of support for pro-
6   grams or projects, related to elder abuse, neglect, and
7   exploitation, assisted by State funds shall not be re-
8   duced below the level provided during the twelve
9   months preceding the date of the enactment of this
10   Act, and set forth policies and procedures designed to
11   assure that Federal funds made available under this
12   Act for any fiscal year will be so used as to supple-
13   ment and, to the extent practicable, increase the level
14   of State funds which would, in the absence of Federal
15   funds, be available for such programs and projects; and

16   (I) provide for dissemination of information to the
17   general public with respect to the problems . of elder
18   abuse, neglect, and exploitation, and the facilities and
19   with respect to prevention and treatment methods
20   available to combat instances of elder abuse, neglect,
21   and exploitation.

22   (c) Assistance provided pursuant to this section shall not
23 be available for construction of facilities; however, the Secre-
24 tary is authorized to supply assistance for the lease or rental
25 of facilities where adequate facilities are not otherwise avail-

1 able, and for repair or minor remodeling or alteration of
2 existing facilities.

3   (d) The Secretary shall establish criteria designed to
4 achieve equitable distribution of assistance under this section
5 among the States, among geographic areas of the Nation,
6 and among rural and urban areas. To the extent possible,
7 citizens of each State shall receive assistance from at least
8 one project under this section.

9 AUTHORIZATION

10   SEC. 5. There are hereby authorized to be appropriated
11 such funds as may be necessary to carry out the purposes of
12 this Act.

DIRECTORY OF STATE OFFICES RESPONSIBLE FOR ADULT PROTECTIVE SERVICES

ALABAMA
State Department of Pensions
and Security
Bureau of Adult Services
64 North Union Street
Montgomery, Alabama 36130

ALASKA
Division of Social Services
Department of Health and Social
Services, Pouch H-05
Juneau, Alaska 99811

ARIZONA
Aging and Adult Administration
1400 West Washington
Phoenix, Arizona 85007

ARKANSAS
Adult Protective Services
Donaghey Building, Rm. 1428
Little Rock, Arkansas 72201

CALIFORNIA
Department of Social Services
Adult PROTECTIVE Supportive
Services Bureau
744 P Streetm N,S. 5-141
Sacramento, California 95814

COLORADO
Colorado State Department of
Social Services
Adult Programs
1575 Sherman
Denver, Colorado 80203

CONNECTICUT
State of Connecticut
Department on Aging
90 Washington Street
Hartford, Connecticut

DELAWARE
Department of Health and
Social Services
New Castle, Delaware 19720

DISTRICT OF COLUMBIA
Protective Services for Adults
Room 613
122 C Street, N. W.
Washington, D. C. 20001

FLORIDA
Aging and Adult Services Program
Office
1317 Winewood Blvd.
Tallahassee, Florida 32301

GEORGIA
Division of Family and Children's
Services
Social Services Section
618 Ponce de Leon Avenue
Atlanta, Georgia 30308

HAWAII
Social Services Intake Unit
1149 Bethel Street, Room 400
Honolulu, Hawaii 96813

IDAHO
State of Idaho
Division of Welfare
Statehouse
Boise, Idaho 83720

ILLINOIS
State Agency on Aging
421 E. Capitol Avenue
Springfield, Ill. 62706

INDIANA
Commission on Aging and Aged
Graphic Arts Building
215 North Senate Avenue
Indianapolis, Indiana 46202

IOWA
Bureau of Adult Services
Hoover State Office Building
Des Moines, Iowa

KANSAS
Adult Services Section
State Department of Social Services
Biddle Building, 1st Floor
2700 West 6th
Topeka, Kansas 66606

KENTUCKY
Department for Human Resources
Division for Aging Services
Alternate Care Branch
275 E. Maine Street, 6th Floor W.
Frankfort, Kentucky 40601

LOUISIANA
Division of Evaluation and Services
P.O. Box 3318
Baton Rouge, Louisiana 70821

MAINE
Adult Protective Services
Department of Human Services Bureau
of Resources Development, Station 11
State House
Augusta, Maine 04333

MARYLAND
State Social Services Administration
Adult Protective Services
11 South Street
Baltimore, Maryland 21212

MASSACHUSETTS
Department of Social Services
11th Floor
150 Causeway Street
Boston, Massachusetts 02114

MICHIGAN
Office of Adult and Family
  Community Services
Adult Protective Services Division
300 South Capitol Avenue
P.O. Box 30037, Suite 707
Commerce Center Building
  Lansing, Michigan 48910

MINNESOTA
State of Minnesota
Department of Public Welfare
Centennial Office Building
St. Paul, Minnesota 55155

MISSISSIPPI
Department of Public Welfare
Jackson, Mississippi

MISSOURI
Missouri Division of Aging
P.O. Box 570
Broadway Office Building
Jefferson City, Missouri 65102

MONTANA
Dept. of Social and Rehabilitative
  Services
Social Services Division
Box 4210
Helena, Montana 59601

NEBRASKA
Division of Social Services
Adult Service Unit
Nebraska Department of Public
  Welfare
Lincoln, Nebraska 68509

NEVADA
Nevada State Welfare Division
251 Jeanell Drive
Carson City, Nevada 89710

NEW HAMPSHIRE
Division of Welfare
Bureau of Adult Services
Haven Drive
Concord, New Hampshire

NEW JERSEY
Dept. of Human Services
Div. of Youth and Family Services
Trenton, New Jersey 08625

NEW MEXICO
Field Services Bureau
Social Services Division
Human Services Department
P.O. Box 2348
Santa Fe, New Mexico 87503

NEW YORK
New York State Dept. of Social
  Services
Aging Services Section
40 North Pearl St.
Albany, New York 12243

NORTH CAROLINA
North Carolina Division of Social
  Services
325 North Salisbury Street
Raleigh, North Carolina 27611

NORTH DAKOTA
County Social Service Boards

OHIO
Bureau of Adult Services
Ohio Department of Public Welfare
30 East Broad Street
Columbus, Ohio 43215

OKLAHOMA
Department of Human Services
Division of Services to Adults and Families
P.O. Box 25352
Oklahoma City, Oklahoma 73125

OREGON
Adult and Family Services
Department of Human Resources
400 Publis Services Building
Salem, Oregon

PENNSYLVANIA
Department of Public Welfare
Room 533
Health and Welfare Building
Harrisburg, Pennsylvania 17120

RHODE ISLAND
Family and Adult Services
600 New London Avenue
Cranston, Rhode Island 02920

SOUTH CAROLINA
Adult Services Division
Adult Protective Services Unit
State Department of Social Services
Box 1520
Columbia, South Carolina 29202

SOUTH DAKOTA
Office of Adult Services
Kneip Building, Illinois Street
Pierre, South Dakota 57501

TENNESSEE
Tennessee Department of Human Services
Division of Social Services
Protective Services for Adults
111-19 7th Avenue North
Nashville, Tennessee 37203

TEXAS
Alternate Care for Aged and Disabled
   Adults Division
Texas Department of Human Resources
P.O. Box 2960
Austin, Texas 78769

UTAH
State Division of Aging
150 West North Temple #326
P.O. Box 2500
Salt Lake City, Utah 84103

VERMONT
Department of Health
60 Main Street
Burlington, Vermont 05401

VIRGINIA
Virginia State Department of Welfare
8007 Discovery Drive
Richmond, Virginia 23288

WASHINGTON
Bureau of Aging
OB-43G
Olympia, Washington 98504

WEST VIRGINIA
All Welfare Department Area Offices

WISCONSIN
Adult Service Units in 72 counties

WYOMING
Wyoming Department of Health and
   Social Services
Division of Public Assistance and
   Social Services
Hathaway Building
Cheyenne, Wyoming 82002

THE NATURE OF ELDER ABUSE: CASE HISTORIES*

The notion that many sons and daughters are purposely and repeatedly abusing their parents is something which is alien to the American spirit. Most people in the United States would be skeptical that the practice exists on anything but an extremely limited scale. Over the past few years, however, there have been an increasing number of studies within the academic community which suggest that the problem is far more important and widespread than has been realized to date.

It was these reports and studies which caused the House Select Committee on Aging to begin holding hearings on the subject of elder abuse. Elder abuse is defined simply as the physical, sexual, psychological or financial abuse of the elderly or otherwise causing the deprivation of their human rights by their relatives or caretakers.

Early hearings by the Committee were for the purpose of exploring the parameters of the problem. It was assumed that to the extent that there was a problem, it would be handled by the States. This assumption was wrong.

The Committee hearings quickly served to reinforce the findings of Committee surveys which concluded elder abuse was a hidden and serious problem. Evidence was received which indicated elder abuse was a matter of growing social importance and that most of the States have not acted to protect the best interests of the elderly. Indeed, in the face of the assertion that elder abuse cases may be equal in size and scope with child abuse cases, the States continue, with rare exceptions, to concentrate their funds almost exclusively to deal with child abuse. Moreover, it is obvious that there is a void in State statutes with respect to protections and services for the abused elderly.

This section of the report makes difficult reading. Hundreds of examples are provided from the Committee files. As noted, the examples are meant to be illustrative, not exhaustive. These shocking examples of the abuse of the elderly by their loved ones are current and virtually all the States are represented. The States which have given the matter of elder abuse the most attention are overrepresented in these examples. State officials predicted to the Committee that as they begin to devote more of their resources to the problem they will undoubtedly uncover hundreds and thousands of additional examples.

The examples which are set forth in this section are entered because this is a way to prove the depth and scope of this serious problem. The Committee does not mean to suggest in this report that the States should cut back on their protection to children; rather, it is suggested that they increase their protection to elders.

Some of the examples below are classics in the history of man's inhumanity to man. The fact that the preperators are most often tied to the abused by blood makes the examples all the more horrible. Some of these abuses which took place in the privacy of the homes of the elderly rival horrors which have come to the public eye from nursing

*Source: "Elder Abuse" (An Examination of a Hidden Problem), *A Report*, Select Committee on Aging, U.S. House of Representatives, 9th Congress, First Session (1981). Comm. Pub. No. 97-277.

homes. Sometimes, as will be seen below, nursing homes provide the refuge for battered and abused elderly. This is not to excuse nursing home abuses which still happen all too frequently but it is enlightening to learn that nursing home operators are sometimes part of the solution instead of always the culprits in this very real human drama concerning the care of the aged.

What follows are examples of abuse which the Committee has received from a number of different sources. Most of the examples come in response to the Committee's several questionnaires to police chiefs, protective service workers, visiting nurse associations and the like. Many examples were received from the states and in correspondence sent to individual members of the Committee.

It should be understood that there is no uniform state definition for the series of abuses the Committee has termed elder abuse. As noted above, these abuses are suffered by senior citizens at the hands of their relatives or caretakers. Caretakers are unrelated individuals placed in a role of providing care and services to the aged usually because the seniors have no other relatives living or who will accept this responsibility. By definition elder abuse involves a pattern or practice of abuse rather than a single isolated incident.

The categories of abuse which are set forth below include physical abuse which consists of two sub-categories, deliberate physical violence and negligence, sexual abuse, financial abuse, and psychological abuse. A separate category—abuse or abrogation of rights is included to show the extent to which older Americans are being deprived of the basic rights which are secured for all citizens by the Constitution and the Bill of Rights. Finally, there is a section on self-abuse which may seem out of place in the context of a report on elder abuse as defined above. However, the examples which are included are by way of recognizing that all of the above abuses combined and perpetrated on the elderly can have a destructive effect on personality. Individuals with a diminished sense of self-worth may not take proper care of themselves or may take active means to end their lives. The high incidence of suicide among the elderly is testimony to what the consequences of familial abuse may become. Obviously, there are other motives for suicide among the elderly than elder abuse and most old people who do not look after their needs cannot do so because of physical infirmities; however, the chapter seeks to identify cases where elder abuse is the precipitating factor triggering either active or passive self abuse.

It is difficult to know just how many horrible examples to include in this report to make the point that the problem is widespread and needs attention. The Committee decided upon a compromise which involves limiting the number in the text which follows below but including additional examples in footnotes at the end of this chapter for those who desire more case histories.

A number of commonalities quickly emerge from the abuses cases reprinted below. Many of the abusers had alcohol or drug-related problems. The son and son-in-law was the most likely abuser and women of advanced age were the most likely victims. Even though the abuses were protracted in nature, they were seldom reported by the victims and their family members. As noted above, the following cases are merely illustrative of the general problem; they are typical of those found in Committee files.

Physical abuse is conduct of violence which results in bodily harm, or mental distress. It can include assault—putting the elderly in fear of violence—at one end of the spectrum all the way to murder and mayhem at the other end of the spectrum. Physical abuse can be either active or passive. Passive abuse is known as negligence; active abuse includes all manner of aggression against a loved one.

DELIBERATE PHYSICAL INJURY

The Committee received hundreds of examples of the deliberate physical injury of senior citizens perpetrated by their relatives. This intentional effort to cause harm to another includes beatings, murder, mayhem and false imprisonment—the unjustified denial of another's freedom of movement. Examples include:

● An elder District of Columbia person, who lived with a daughter-in-law, was often found with injuries which could not result from falls. The older person was not given medication and was sometimes found dehydrated. She was sent to the hospital on one such occasion where death resulted.

● Another District of Columbia woman 80-years-old was found beaten to death and her acting caregiver was charged with the homicide. Detectives said the motive was robbery.

● A complete bed-care patient in D.C. was murdered, by the son-when the patient's wife was admitted to the hospital with mental problems.

● A 70-year-old woman from the District of Columbia was routinely victimized by her caretaker who started work as her maid. The caretaker forced the woman to turn over all of her money, opened all her mail, removed the phone from her room and denied her any contact with the outside world. The woman was repeatedly tied to the bed with wire and left alone for long periods of time. The caretaker beat her and pushed the woman at reckless speeds in her wheel chair causing serious injury to her. The woman twice suffered a broken hip and once a broken clavicle in this manner. The caretaker took the woman's car, personal possessions and about $5,000 in cash. Eventually, the former maid was indicted for extortion, false imprisonment, first degree grand theft and misrepresenting herself as a licensed nurse.

● The Atlanta police also reported that an older woman was attacked by her 30-year-old son with a butcher knife. He lives in her home, is capable of working but will not. She therefore continues to support him.

● Florida also reported an incident where an elderly woman with a heart condition was being routinely abused by her 15-year-old grandson. On one occasion, he threw a suitcase at her, hitting her head. She also had bruises on her arms from beating. He hit her only in places where it would do no damage according to the grandmother. The grandson did not really know why he hit his grandmother except that she made him angry.

123

- A 73-year-old Florida man was indicted for assault and battery of his 78-year-old sister. Repeatedly, he abused her and tied her to a straight back chair in his back yard where she sat in all kinds of weather. Neighbors and the police intervened time after time but the events were repeated. Once they placed the sister in a nursing home but the brother removed her threatening to kill anyone who would separate him from his sister. Since the brother had just completed a jail sentence for manslaughter, his threats were taken seriously. Eventually, the woman was removed to an emergency shelter to prevent the brother from continuing the conduct described above or of killing his sister which he had threatened.

- Illinois supplied the Committee with a number of physical abuse cases which had come to their attention:

    - —A 19-year-old woman confessed to torturing her 81-year-old father and chaining him to a toilet for 7 days. She also hit him with a hammer when he was asleep. After she made him weak enough, she chained his legs together.

    - —An 81-year-old woman was repeatedly beaten by her 8-year-old grandson until there were black and blue marks across her face and entire body. The boy apparently had encouragement from other family members.

- An 80-year-old Indianapolis female was struck on the forehead with a telephone by her 15-year-old grandson, after he had ripped it out of the wall. He had struck his grandmother several times before.

- The Indianapolis police reported that an elderly male was stabbed by his 23-year-old son. The son had been locked up three times for this same type of incident, and when the elderly victim did not show up for court appearances, the cases were dismissed.

- A widow in Iowa, living with her son, was hospitalized for hypothermia and pneumonia. She was found to have bruises on her left pubic region, right hip, face, shoulders and upper abdomen. She had scar-like lesions on her arms, hands and an open ulcer on her shin. A relative confirmed parent abuse by the son and indicated a pattern of abuse over the years. A visit to the home revealed that it was very old, inadequately heated, dirty, and unsafe. The toilet was inaccessible to the client because of unsafe stairs.

- An 81-year-old woman in Ohio was brought to the emergency room by her daughter and son-in-law with whom she had lived for the past 5 years. They said that she had fallen and sustained injuries. Physicians diagnosed severe head injuries including a fractured skull which could not have been caused by a fall. Caseworkers confirmed a pattern of abuse noting that the family had experienced much stress in caring for the needs of this demanding 81–year-old woman.

- A 92-year-old Massachusetts woman was admitted to a hospital emergency room severely beaten, and with a skull fracture. She died a week later. A son and daughter-in-law, with whom the bedridden woman lived, are considered suspects in her death.

- A Massachusetts grandmother's death resulted when her grand-son allegedly shot her then apparently burned the house down to cover up the crime. It was only when the medical examiner examined the victim that the gunshot wound was discovered. The case is being prosecuted under a criminal indictment. It was later learned that the grandmother had been physically assaulted by her grandson on several occasions in past years.

- A Massachusetts physician reported a case in which a badly bruised woman was accompanied by her middle-age daughter who pleaded, "Please help me doctor; I'm beating my mother."

- In Massachusetts, a 95-year-old woman living with her grand-children complained to a visiting nurse that when she asked for help in getting to the bathroom during the night, her grand-daughter's husband responds by putting a pillow over her face or chaining her to the bedpost.

- Missouri reported that a 71-year-old woman lived with her 36-year-old son and 39-year-old daughter, both of whom were retarded. There was documentation of several minor physical attacks by the son. The third attack was major and required that the mother be hospitalized because of her critical condition. She remained in the hospital for four weeks and was then trans-ferred to a foster home placement. Her absence from the house-hold led to the eventual institutionalization of these two adult children.

- In Michigan, a 73-year-old woman complained to the police that her 35-year-old son had been beating her for 2 years since her husband had died. Eventually, the elderly woman contacted a social service worker. She was in bad physical shape—her arms and face were bruised, her wrist was broken and she required several stitches in her head. Her son was found to be mentally ill and was committed.

- Mrs. M. was dependent on her slightly retarded son. Occasion-ally, he became annoyed with her and took his revenge. He would step on her catheter, pulling it out. Once he ran a wheelchair over her foot and fractured a bone. Another time he dropped her and broke her hip.

- An elderly woman from New Hampshire was brought to a hos-pital emergency room by her caregiver boyfriend. She had a fractured shoulder, had been punched in the face and knocked unconscious, and her upper ribs were black and blue. The house where the patient, caregiver boyfriend and a second male lived was filthy and alcohol bottles were scattered throughout the residence.

NEGLIGENCE

Negligence can be defined as conduct which is careless; it is the breach of a duty which results in injury to a person or in a violation of rights. There is ample evidence of negligence by relatives and care-takers with devastating consequences to the helpless elderly. This sec-tion of this report details a few of these examples collected by the Committee from across the country. These abuses took place within the past few years. The list below is meant to be illustrative rather than comprehensive.

- In South Carolina, a 79-year-old woman who was recuperating from a stroke was kept in an unheated porch attached to her daughter's $90,000 house. The family refused to buy soft foods and to otherwise accept responsibility for the victim who became dehydrated and required hospitalization.

- In the same State, a 68-year-old woman living with her daughter was found by a caseworker in conditions of unspeakable squalor. The woman was kept in an unheated portion of the house where the temperature was measured at less than 20 degrees. When found, the woman had eight soiled blankets piled over her head to keep her warm and the urine from her catheter was frozen. She was also found to be malnourished. She developed pneumonia and was hospitalized. Upon discharge, authorities had her placed in a nursing home.

- Washington State reported that they were alerted by concerned neighbors who noticed social security checks being delivered monthly and yet they had not seen a woman they knew as "granny" for over a year. Caseworkers arrived at the home where the woman lived with her daughter and grandsons but could not approach the home because of vicious dogs. They returned with the police and representatives of the humane society. The elderly woman was found locked in an upstairs room, dirty, disheveled, incontinent and malnourished. The victim requested that she be relocated to a nursing home.

- An elderly woman in New Jersey living with her daughter and son-in-law was systematically neglected. She was left at home all day without food. At night her potty chair and walker were removed so that she could not get up and go to the bathroom. Her personal correspondence was withheld and her telephone calls intercepted. One day the woman fell and was left alone to lie for about eight hours on the floor with a broken hip. When interviewed, the daughter said that she wanted her mother dead so that there would be no more problems. The woman was placed in a nursing home by authorities.

- An elderly paraplegic Arkansas woman had been hospitalized three times for surgery. Her husband refused to place her in a nursing home because he wanted continued access to his wife's Federal Supplementary Security Income check. The man was an alcoholic and used the proceeds to support his habit. It was learned by investigators that during the day he would load his wife into the back of his pickup truck and leave her there while he would go to drink beer at a local poolhall. During the woman's subsequent fourth hospital stay, the husband died in a fire which broke out in the couple's house trailer. The woman was then placed in a long-term care facility.

- In Washington, an 84-year-old woman, terminally ill with cancer, was refused proper medical attention by her grandson who did not want the woman's property and income dissipated by doctor and hospital payments. The woman was found in tremendous pain, living in truly wretched conditions. The victim was transferred to a nursing home where she died a few weeks later.

- Caseworkers in West Virginia were alerted that an 80-year-old couple might be having problems. Upon investigation they found the husband ill to the point of being comatose. The man was described as "unable to respond, barely breathing with eyes glazed." The wife was exhausted and distraught from trying to care for her husband to the point where her mental condition was unstable. The wife would not allow authorities to remove the man to a hospital for treatment. She charged them with engaging in a plot to take her husband away from her. Caseworkers contacted the couple's daughter to assist them in persuading the wife that the man needed attention. They were unsuccessful and the husband died two days thereafter.

- An 83-year-old Ohio woman, in the care of her daughter, was bitten by a dog. The daughter neglected to seek appropriate attention but simply bandaged her mother's arm. No effort was made to locate the dog or to learn if it had rabies. Three days later, a nurse in a day care center noticed that the arm was badly swollen and infected and called the daughter for permission to institute treatment or take the woman to a physician. The daughter was resistant. The nurse was insistent and sometime later, the daughter agreed to have her mother treated at the emergency room of the local hospital. The attending physician gave her a tetanus shot and ordered antibiotics and antiseptic dressings. The woman died one week thereafter and it is believed by authorities that initial neglect of the dog bite wound was a contributing factor in her death.

- Social workers in North Carolina found a 70-year-old woman lying in her own urine and feces in a house with a horrendous, stifling odor. It was clear that the woman had been neglected by her daughter. The mother was malnourished and suffered 2nd and 3rd degree burns on her knees and thighs which were uncared for. Caseworkers commented the daughter "showed absolutely no desire to care for her mother."

- An Ohio woman with severe rheumatoid arthritis was found suffering from severe malnutrition and dehydration. On several occasions, she required hospitalization as a consequence of neglect. During one admission, maggots were found over the woman's entire body. No relative would accept responsibility for her; however, when social services workers tried to remove her to a nursing home they were blocked from doing so by the family.

- In Iowa, an elderly man suffered two strokes and was left totally dependent on his wife for his care. The elderly wife suffered from arthritis and diabetes. Under the burden of the couple's financial problems, she became easily fatigued and soon became depressed. She admitted to caseworkers that she deliberately withheld therapy and medication needed by her husband. She stated that she spent little time in his room because she could not bear to look at him in his present condition. The woman said that because of guilt feelings and the likely depletion of the couple's few assets, she did not want to place her husband in a nursing home. She stated that she wished her husband would die.

- A 67-year-old West Virginia woman living with her alcoholic son suffered a stroke which left her paralyzed on her right side. The woman also suffered from cancer. After hospitalization, she was returned to the care of her son. The woman slept on an old cot with no bed linens and had no way to bathe. Caseworkers said the woman seemed afraid to talk in front of her son, who answered all of her questions for her. The woman would not agree to a nursing home even though she had acquired two huge bedsores. Several weeks later, caseworkers were finally successful in removing her from these deplorable conditions to a nursing home.

- An 80-year-old South Carolina woman, crippled with arthritis and too obese to get around, was left in the care of her 50-year-old son. The son cashed her social security checks and tied her to the bed and padlocked the bedroom door every day before he went out. He would leave a few saltines and water within reach when he left.

- Another mother in South Carolina, age 76, was left in the care of her son. The woman suffered from senility, arthritis, and could not stand up alone. The son would leave her alone for two and three days at a time with only a baby bottle full of water at her bedside. When caseworkers investigated, the son resisted their efforts to place her in a home. He said he would do better by his mother. A month later caseworkers returned to find the woman in the same condition as before: malnourished, bedridden, filthy and ill. She was placed in a nursing home.

- In Iowa, caseworkers found an elderly woman seriously ill, delirious with fever, in a urine-soaked bed. The Sheriff's Department arranged hospitalization against the spouse's will. The husband refused nursing home placement following the hospital stay and the woman returned to the unsanitary conditions, improper diet, poor medication supervision and improper catheter care.

- In West Virginia, an 82-year-old widow with a broken hip, poor circulation and a heart condition was left in the care of her 52-year-old son. The son was a former mental patient who left his mother for several days at a time without food or medication. The son kept loaded guns in the house and would not allow neighbors to visit. The son was finally placed in a State mental institution with the help of neighbors who expressed the fear that they and the 82-year-old woman would be in great danger when the son is released.

- Caseworkers in Colorado were called in to investigate reports that an elderly man was not properly caring for his wife. It was learned that the woman had terminal cancer and that the husband at times would withhold medication and medical treatments as prescribed by physicians and institute a regimen of over-the-counter medications. Caseworkers had the woman placed in a hospital but the man would have her discharged back to his care at home. Finally, the Department of Social Services was given guardianship responsibilities for the woman and saw to her care with appropriate medical and nursing services until her death.

- North Carolina investigators found that a woman was keeping her elderly husband and mother-in-law captive in the upstairs of the couple's home. The upstairs portion of the house was described as laden with feces while the downstairs, where the wife

lived, was clean smelling and fresh. The man was found to have
developed bedsores from lying in his own waste.

- An elderly Washington, D.C. woman was tied in bed, deprived of
food and stripped of her financial assets by a granddaughter
with whom she was living. Pressures among the family members
prevented any action from taking place. Finally, the woman was
hospitalized for dehydration and malnutrition.

- Louisiana officials reported finding a 92-year-old woman neglected
by her niece and nephew with whom she lived. The woman was
frequently left alone without food and water, not given a bath
for a month and suffered from fleas. Caseworkers reported the
woman was tricked into changing her will so that upon her death,
her home and all her property would go to the niece and nephew.

- A South Carolina woman, age 72, suffering from chronic brain
syndrome, was left in the care of her son who gave her a room in
the rear of his rented house. Caseworkers reported finding her
dehydrated from time to time usually lying on a wet mattress
with a chicken leg or a half of a banana in her hand. Apparently,
the woman was incapable of raising her hand to her mouth without help. The son resisted efforts to place the woman in a nursing
home until ordered to do so by a physician. The woman died
within one week of the transfer.

- A 71-year-old Missouri woman was brought into the hospital
emergency room in filthy condition: hair matted and covered
with feces, bedsores over her body and in a comatose condition.
Hospital officials said that neglect was the cause of the woman's
condition. The woman had been hospitalized previously for
"suspect incidences" and there was evidence of head injuries of
"unknown origin." The husband claimed he did not know how
sick his wife was. Caseworkers learned that the man was reluctant to seek nursing home placement because his wife's income
would be lost to him. The patient was admitted to a nursing home
because of the assistance of social workers.

- Another woman in Missouri, age 77, who had suffered a recent
stroke and was bedridden was left in the care of her only son
who was in his early 40's and on welfare. The son was a diabetic
and suffered from asthma. The two people lived in a rowhouse
confining themselves to the top floor bedrooms, cooking on a hot
plate, and washing dishes in the bathtub. Since the son had 20 to
30 cats, the house was extremely filthy and filled with cat feces.
Although many agencies tried to intervene the occupants would
permit no one to clean the house. The son was married about four
or five years, although he intimated that the marriage was never
consummated. The daughter-in-law, who had since remarried,
still visited her mother-in-law. The son owned two or three
motorcycles and had an extensive gun collection plus a room full
of World War II mementos. Occasionally, he worked as a drummer in a nightclub and was frequently known to become drunk
and violent. He had often beaten his mother who contacted the
police when he did so. The police, aware of the problem, were
often able to calm the son. At other times, he threatened to kill
her and stated he wished she were dead. Although she was frequently ill and required constant health care, health aides sent

to the house were threatened by physical violence by the son and were afraid to return.

- Louisiana officials verified that a 73-year-old woman was neglected and exploited by her granddaughter. The victim was blind and yet she was left alone, not fed, allowed to lie in her own urine and feces on a dirty mattress. The victim's money was taken by the granddaughter who convinced the elderly woman that if she entered a nursing home she would starve.

- An elderly Maryland woman was confined to a cellar by her daughter-in-law who was charged with her care and supervision. The woman received little care and had evidence of cuts and bruises when visited by caseworkers. The daughter stated that she did not want her mother to mess up the house.

- A 70-year-old woman in the District of Columbia was admitted to the hospital for malnutrition and dehydration. She had been living alone, cared for by a neighbor who was paid by a goddaughter of the elderly woman. When the goddaughter stopped paying, the care stopped as well.

- An 88-year-old woman with mental problems was the source of support for her stepgrandson and his girlfriend. At times, she was locked out of the house for extended periods. The stepgrandson refused to cook or clean. Neighbors brought food for her but the man would eat it himself and not share it with the old woman. On several occasions when she was ill, he abandoned the old woman and left her alone. The stepgrandson had purchased only one light bulb for the entire house and yet social workers learned that he sometimes left the front door open, letting in the cold and letting the heat escape.

- In Massachusetts, an 86-year-old woman was on three separate occasions found wandering the neighborhood in a confused state during the winter. She was wearing only nightclothes and slippers. She was totally disoriented. When contacted by authorities, her sons could not agree even on a home health care plan for her. She died six months later.

- An elderly Oklahoma woman who was bedfast was found to be the victim of gross neglect by her grandson. Caseworkers found her bedfast, emaciated, and lying in feces. Attempts to improve conditions failed. Finally, the court was petitioned to authorize involuntary protective services and the woman was relocated to a nursing home.

- A weak, frail elderly New Jersey woman on a salt-free diet was being left alone by her working daughter. The mother was unable to dress herself and was left with only stale bread and canned soup to eat. She was placed in a day care center so she could have daytime activities and care, and remained with the family at night.

- An elderly woman in Massachusetts cared for her schizophrenic son until she fractured her hip. The son then became her caretaker. The house became increasingly disorderly with broken plumbing which was not repaired and excrement was dumped in the yard. Two months after the protective service agency took the case, the woman died. The son then cleaned, repaired and sold the home.

130

Sexual abuse of the elderly by their relatives is a gruesome subject, It needs no further definition and a few examples are sufficient to make the point.

- In the District of Columbia, an 80-year-old woman, a paraplegic, had been sexually abused over a 6-year period by her son-in-law, who beat her with a hammer when she refused his advances.

- A 69-year-old woman from Iowa in day care complained of abdominal pain and vaginal bleeding. She revealed she had been raped by her brother-in-law, with whom she and her husband had been living after being evicted from their home. After reporting the problem, she filed charges against her brother-in-law who was jailed and is awaiting trial.

- Iowa also reported that an arthritic, slightly obese but otherwise healthy woman lived with her daughter and 22-year-old grandson who reportedly physically and sexually abused her. The daughter admitted there was familial conflict and wanted her mother to move. The mother was turning over $300 of her $320 monthly Social Security check to the daughter.

- New Jersey reported that a lady of about 74 was assaulted physically and sexually by her son-in-law. The daughter was fully aware of the ongoing situation, and warned her mother not so say anything for if she did she would be made homeless. Neighbors and relatives reported the case to protective services.

FINANCIAL EXPLOITATION

Financial exploitation involves the theft or conversion of money or anything of value belonging to the elderly by their relatives or caretakers. Sometimes, this theft or misappropriation is accomplished by force—sometimes at gun point. In other cases, it is accomplished by stealth through deceit, misrepresentation and fraud. In most instances, the loss of property by the elderly is immediate but in a few instances involving undue influence in the writing of wills, greedy family members have been willing to wait a few months or even years to acquire the property of a loved one.

In its inquiry, the Committee developed literally thousands of examples which fall into the category of financial exploitation. As is noted from other parts of this report, financial abuse usually is accompanied by physical and psychological abuse. The examples provided below are merely illustrative of the problem. They range from armed robbery of the elderly by their loved ones to larceny of their personal possessions to exotic schemes to defraud them of literally anything of value.

One of the most heartbreaking series of examples involves the elderly who lived independently until an injury or illness necessitated a stay in the hospital. Upon discharge from the hospital, many older Americans have learned to their chagrin that their families have literally sold their homes out from under them. Equally heartbreaking are cases where family members have their loved ones committed to a public institution as a means of obtaining their property.

It became apparent to the Committee that to some extent, Federal policy under Medicare/Medicaid and the Supplementary Security

Income program encourage the financial exploitation of the elderly. Generally, the exploitation revolves around the decision to place an older person in a nursing home or related institution. Since Medicare pays for only about 2 percent of the nation's total $17 billion nursing home bill, the elderly must pay these expenses themselves or look to their families. With average charges in American nursing homes running in excess of $12,000 a year and given the fact that no insurance can be found which will pay more than a modest amount of this bill, more and more families have been looking for ways to qualify their loved ones for Medicaid, the welfare nursing home program which is available without limit to the poor. Families have learned that if the elderly divest themselves of their resources and income, they will become eligible for Medicaid.

Many family members rationalize that it is a pity to waste money (even if it belongs to the elderly) on old people near death and that it is somehow compounding the problem to give this money to what they call greedy nursing home owners. For this reason, family members have taken money or property belonging to the elderly and then represented to State Medicaid workers with a straight face that the senior has no property, thus qualifying for Medicaid.

With respect to SSI—a program of cash grants to the poor elderly from the Federal government, the problem is caused by a provision in the law which reduces SSI payments by one-third if the senior lives with related individuals. There is also a provision which bars the receipt of SSI funds for most individuals housed in public institutions. What this means is that more and more old people are being entered in the Federal SSI rolls instead of being taken care of at home. The fact that public institutions are generally unavailable means the elderly are increasingly being placed in private for-profit boarding homes. While the subject of boarding homes was incidental to this study, the Committee could not help but be moved by the tremendous number of abuses which were reported in boarding homes. While the matter merits further study, it would appear that boarding homes have replaced nursing homes as the premier havens for institutionalized abuse of the elderly in America. Indeed, a number of victims of boarding home abuse and of abuse at home by loved ones have found nursing homes a pleasant change by comparison. Examples of financial exploitation of the elderly follow:

● In Arizona, an 88-year-old bedridden, mentally incompetent woman who was being cared for by a young relative was placed in the cheapest available boarding home. Her stay at the home was paid for with the woman's social security check of $300 a month. Thereafter, the young relative began to spend the victim's $20,000 life savings. When caseworkers investigated, the victim was found suffering from bedsores and dehydration. In fact, the woman was so dehydrated according to official reports, that her lips were stuck together. Employees of the boarding home would not give the woman fluids because they didn't want her wetting the bedsheets. After an investigation, the victim was removed to a nursing home where she received proper nursing and medical care.

● In the same State, a woman who had worked for over 30 years and who enjoyed a liberal pension, suffered two broken hips at the age of 88. An acquaintance arranged for her to be placed in an unlicensed boarding home. Within two weeks, the owners had either forged the victim's name to checks or had forced her to sign over $2,300 in checks to them. The investigation revealed that the woman was purposely overmedicated in order to keep her in a stupor. The woman had numerous stocks and bonds which apparently had been misappropriated. Social workers hired an attorney to institute legal proceedings to recover funds inappropriately taken and moved the victim to a licensed nursing home where she is reportedly receiving excellent care.

- Also in Arizona, an 84-year-old World War I veteran with a diagnosis of congestive heart failure came under the influence of a "friend" who obtained the old man's power of attorney and opened joint bank accounts with him. The "friend" represented that the man had no relatives. Investigators learned of the case when the man was brought to the emergency room of a local hospital. The old man was malnourished, dehydrated and maggots had infested under his skin. Investigators learned that approximately $20,000 had been taken. Relatives were located in Florida and Michigan but they refused to accept responsibility for the man so a guardian was appointed by the court to revoke the power of attorney and recover the man's assets. Both the old man and State social workers were physically threatened but ultimately they were successful in recovering an automobile and much of the other financial assets. The man was placed in a county nursing home.

- California officials report that an 87-year-old widow in frail health and generally confined to a wheelchair, unable to care for her day-to-day needs, was allegedly the victim of physical and financial abuse from 1974 through 1980. A nurse companion who was also her conservator and three children depleted her financial resources by more than $300,000 while depriving the woman of proper medical attention, food or clothing. Caseworkers helped the woman to institute legal proceedings.

- Mrs. Z, then age 86, lived with her sister, age 84, in a home they shared in California. After a stroke, she was hospitalized and comatose for 6 months. Part of her convalescence was in a nursing home. Prior to recovery, her sister was placed in another nursing home by a former caretaker, Sue, representing herself as probate conservator for both sisters. She had filed copies of conservatorship petitions in the sisters medical records, then had withdrawn the original petitions from the court calendar before they were legally recorded. She also got title to the sisters home with a quit claim deed signed by both sisters, had wills signed by the sisters naming her as heir in case either sister pre-deceased the other. Both wills named her as executor. Mrs. Z's signatures on the documents were dated during her comatose period. When Mrs. Z regained consciousness, and fully recovered her mental and physical faculties, she began asking questions about her affairs and possessions, including jewelry Sue was wearing. She was told Sue was in charge with full legal authority. Mrs. Z was not to contact her sister, who was also angry at Sue. The sister lapsed into total mental confusion and died 3 years after nursing home placement. Before her death, the case was referred to adult protective services because of a Medicaid-pension problem and subsequent checking of court records revealed Sue had no legal authority or conservatorship. Mrs. Z denied ever having made a will, signing over her house, giving power of attorney, or giving her possessions to Sue. At this time, her memory was unimpaired except for the comatose period. After 6 years of legal procedures, Mrs. Z, at age 92, recovered partial possession of her home and a few personal possessions. A public guardian was correctly appointed for her and was also conservator for her sister until the latter's death.

- California officials also report that they discovered that a number of elderly men had been extorted by an attractive young woman. They discovered the scheme following the death of a 72-year-old retired man who had loaned the woman about $2,000. It was learned that there was no repayment of the loan, that the woman was an alcoholic and an opportunist who employed various methods of getting money from lonely elderly men.

- An elderly man from the District of Columbia, living with his son, was unable to handle his financial affairs because of debilitating illness. Believing his bank balance to be $10,000, he wrote a check for a couple hundred dollars and was overdrawn. He later learned that his son had withdrawn money without telling him.

- Officials in the District of Columbia report several cases where relatives, including daughters, granddaughters, and nephews, entered the homes of the ill elderly when they were being hospitalized, and removed cash and possessions in anticipation of the senior citizen's death. In a similar case, a 90-year-old woman who lived independently in her own home until she fractured her hip and was hospitalized, had her home sold out from under her by her family who then had her placed in a nursing home.

- In Atlanta an elderly woman was financially abused by her 30-year-old daughter. The daughter would leave her five children with her mother and disappear for months. She took money from her mother and assaulted her when her mother took exception to her actions. The mother was fearful and too afraid to take action against her daughter.

- Florida investigators report that they discovered that an 82-year-old woman had been fooled into signing a quit claim deed to her property by a daughter whom she trusted. The woman did not know that the papers she signed had the effect of conveying her house and property to her daughter. In addition, the woman was neglected or abused and mistreated by her daughter until caseworkers intervened last year.

- In Florida, a 64-year-old man in poor health was swindled out of his 40 acre orange grove and all his other possessions by a relative he trusted. The relative misrepresented the purpose of the papers and the effect of the man's signature. The man was left with only his social security. He was threatened and abused and given liquor with his medication. "I signed too many papers. I still fear for my life," he told protective service workers.

- Florida protective service workers report a number of incidents which involve family members helping themselves to the possessions of relatives who had been hospitalized. In one case, more than $3,000 was withdrawn from the senior citizen's account by relatives who had obtained the bank book when the victim was too sick to move. In another instance, a 46-year-old daughter, together with the 5-year-old granddaughter, ransacked the home of a senior. In another instance, a son was spending his mother's veterans check to buy drugs and alcohol. A poignant letter to the State from a senior citizen captures the essence of this problem: "Some of us cannot run and hide . . . some of us are very vulnerable to legal trickery. Some of us are too poor to hire a lawyer. The prevailing attitude is why spend the effort on an old person because he or she is going to kick off soon anyway and through that excuse they deny relief or justice. Older people are more afraid to talk back to corrupt bureaucracy because that monolithic conspiracy can very easily tamper with the (income) of the more vulnerable. We must remember older people sometimes own property that other people want without paying for it."

- Florida reports that there are instances where attorneys, by themselves or in collusion with family members, have defrauded the elderly. In one instance, an 80-year-old man lost $50,000 in a confidence scheme then was allegedly tricked into assigning some $11,000 in cash and real estate to an attorney with the hope of recovering the lost funds. The client had to hire a second attorney who withdrew from the case a year and one half later. A judgment was finally obtained against the operators of the confidence scheme who could not be located.

- Florida also reports that a 93-year-old former college professor was kept captive in his own home by his "housekeeper" who brought her family to live in the home. The professor's money was used to pay all the bills, including the cost of a sports car and other luxuries. The man was left alone and neglected. Neighbors intervened after the old man fell and hurt himself. Subsequent investigation proved that his funds had been rapidly depleted. Three lots had been sold without his knowledge. Eventually, a conservator was appointed and he voluntarily entered a nursing home.

- Louisiana reports a 92-year-old woman was mistreated by her niece and nephew. The woman was left alone without food or water, at times going a month or more without a bath. She suffered from fleas and flea bites which were left untreated. It was alleged that she was tricked into giving all of her property, including her home, to her niece and nephew. It is clear they were using the senior's money for their own personal benefit.

- Louisiana also reports several instances where relatives have converted the income of their elderly to their own use. In one case, an adopted son, age 22, helped himself to all of the senior's income, including social security, and used the proceeds to buy alcohol. In another case, a 73-year-old blind woman was neglected by her granddaughter who left her living in squalor while converting the old woman's funds to her own use.

- In Maine, caseworkers had to persuade a reluctant old man to bring suit against his daughter to recover some $24,000 taken from two of his savings accounts.

- Caseworkers in Maryland told the Committee about a 67-year-old widow who was regularly beaten by her 35-year-old son. The widow was forced to turn over all her property and assets to the son who stopped working. When the income money from property had been exhausted, the two subsisted on her $80 a month social security check. The widow did some babysitting to supplement this income.

● The daughter and husband of an elderly nursing home patient were discovered not having told Maryland authorities about the patient's income from social security. The patient had her care paid for by Medicaid which is required by law to be offset by any income which the person may have. When they were required to turn the checks over to the nursing home, they pulled the woman out of the home saying they would care for her at home. The woman is a diabetic and cannot care for her personal needs and yet it is assumed that she is left alone all day since both the husband and daughter work. They were using the social security checks to make their automobile payments.

● In Massachusetts, family members sought a court order to have a nursing home patient's life support systems taken away despite evidence that the man wanted to live. Caseworkers said that financial holdings were at the bottom of the family's efforts to have the man's dialysis treatments ended.

● In the same State, a 68-year-old widow with a heart condition and crippled with arthritis was physically and financially abused by her heroin-addict son. An investigation revealed that the son stole money and sold the woman's property, such as her color television and stereo system. The son also ran up huge bills on the woman's credit cards and incurred other indebtedness. Caseworkers intervened and got the son to move out but the widow refused to press charges or to bring any action to recover her property.

● The Minneapolis Tribune in 1978 reported a number of abuses which involved for-profit estate management corporations who are appointed to sell off the assets of the elderly, usually to allow the proceeds to be applied toward nursing home placement. Following the death of the elderly *, the purpose is usually to convert assets into cash which can be divided among the family members:

   —One case involved Mrs. L., an elderly nursing home patient. The conservator, an estate management corporation, sold her home for $8,400 although it had been appraised for $10,250 earlier that year. The substantially identical home of a neighbor had sold for $17,500 four years earlier. Six months after the sale, Mrs. L.'s house was resold for $19,500. The corporation obtained a generous commission and legal fees for its trouble. Collusion was suspected but never proven between the corporation and the initial purchaser.

   —Mrs. R., age 102 and in a nursing home, was under the conservatorship of an estate management corporation which set the value of her home at $7,800, the sale price of the house which had been appraised at $9,500. The buyer then sold the house for $16,200, more than twice what he paid for it. Mrs. R.'s conservator filed for welfare assistance for his client.

*Similar cases were reported to the Committee by Daphne Krause, Executive Director of the excellent Minneapolis Age and Opportunity Center of Minneapolis, Minn.

—A niece of Mrs. M., an 89-year-old woman, learned that the aunt had been placed in a nursing home and enrolled in Medicaid by a conservator estate management corporation, ostensibly because she had no assets. The niece visited the old woman and found her tied to a chair. The administrator offered the excuse that the aunt could not sit in a chair without support, stating she was uncooperative with therapy. The niece decided to investigate further. She visited the home which had been vacant since her aunt's admission to the nursing home. The house was unlocked. It appeared to have been ransacked. Food was still in the pots. The insurance had lapsed. The niece found about $5,000 in checks and cash that had been hidden in the house. She learned that the conservator had not filed an inventory and appraisal of the estate nor an accounting for assets and expenditures during the term of the conservatorship which was almost 18 months at that point. The niece was able to pay $11,000 in nursing home charges incurred prior to her aunt's being placed on Medicaid. The conservator accused the niece of meddling, insisting that the house would bring only $12,000. The niece sold it for $18,500. The niece paid the conservator legal fees; the corporation resigned and the niece was appointed guardian. In her first accounting, the niece listed her aunt's assets at $53,140 after payment of all bills. The aunt will therefore be able to support herself from this income for several years instead of becoming a ward of the State.

—Mrs. V. who had an estate of approximately $73,000, much of it in stocks and bonds, was placed in a nursing home and a corporation was appointed as her guardian. Following a stroke, the guardian began preparing to sell the home on the rationale that she would never be able to live by herself or otherwise occupy the house again. The house was sold for $12,000, even though it had been appraised for $13,500 a year earlier. Three months later, the house was resold for $17,700 and three years later, it brought $31,600. The original buyer of the home had also bought two other homes of nursing home patients under the conservatorship of the same corporation.

—Mrs. O. was also placed under a conservatorship because she could no longer manage her own affairs. Her son was appointed her guardian in 1975. In March of 1976, he signed a purchase agreement to purchase his mother's home for $26,200. He asked the court to release him as conservator and to appoint a for-profit estate management corporation. The son bought the house, rented it for a few months, and then sold it for $37,000. A Minnesota newspaper investigation showed that this corporation had sold a number of homes belonging to the aged at prices below market value. The study noted that the sale prices are further diminished by closing costs which reduced the owner's benefit from $2,000 to $11,000 per house. In this case, Mrs. O. received only $72.75 from her $30,000 estate and became a welfare (Medicaid) client before her death in 1979.

● An elderly New Jersey man with a monthly pension of $950 and $200,000 savings became ill, was hospitalized with seizures that left him brain injured and partially paralyzed. His caretakers obtained legal power of attorney. Although it was believed by his sisters that he did receive some care, the caretakers took his pension and social security checks, stripped him of his savings and denied him visits from his sisters. The caretakers also sold his car.

- An elderly woman from New Jersey gave her lawyer power of attorney when he told her she was signing something related to the sale of her house. He later tried to borrow money on the woman's bank account while she was still alive. Fifteen months after her death, nothing had been done about the estate and the attorney was still collecting monthly fees as co-executor and legal counsel as stated in her will.

- New Jersey reported a situation where an elderly woman asked a man considered a "pillar of the community" to manage her estate and gave him power of attorney. When she became ill, a home health aide who came to assist her had to buy food out of her own funds for her. The pharmacists were balking at delivering more medication until their long-overdue bills were paid. The aide learned that the woman had sufficient funds to pay her expenses. In fact, she was extremely well-off, but this fact was not known because her conservator was not acting in her best interests.

- New Jersey officials also reported a case where title to a woman's home had been turned over to her son, an attorney, apparently without the woman's knowledge or permission. Caseworkers were unsuccessful in their efforts to restore title of the home because of the unavailability of legal assistance.

- New York reported the case of a 75-year-old woman, widowed, who was in failing health. For this reason, she chose to move into a home where she could receive appropriate care and be close to relatives. Her net worth was $160,000. Instead of moving into the home, she was asked to move into the private residence of a couple in the vicinity as a paying guest. During the next few months, the cancer for which she was being treated, worsened. She also had cataracts and had suffered several strokes. In October 1977, one of the caretakers bought a new foreign automobile with cashier's checks totalling slightly less than $21,000 purchased by the 75-year-old woman. The caretaker claimed the older woman bought it for her as a gift. During the following 9 months that she lived with the caretaker, approximately $89,000 found its way directly to the caretaker and approximately $35,000 disappeared from her estate altogether. Her assets at the time of death were only $40,000.

- In New York, a 79-year-old woman was found missing by a friend. She was discovered to be residing in a boarding home. The older woman was suffering from "chronic brain disease, heart problems, and thyroidtoxicosis." During the period of time she resided in the home, her caretaker had her withdraw $3500 from her bank account with which she purchased $3400 worth of travelers checks which were endorsed by the caretaker and an additional $100 check was made payable to the caretaker's husband. Later, substantial amounts of money were withdrawn from her savings account by the caretaker. Approximately

$80,000 of the older woman's money was sent to Ireland and deposited there in trust for two of the caretaker's children. Prior to the older woman's death, the caretaker and her husband became the proponents of a will drawn during the time the older woman was living with them, revoking a will made approximately a year earlier, leaving the bulk of her estate to them instead of to various relatives. She was apparently acutely ill for days before her death, but received no specific medical treatment for her last illness. The court has voided her last will as the product of fraud and undue influence.

- Also in New York, an attorney was contacted by Mr. and Mrs. X. who claimed to be friends of Mr. C. who was sick and wanted to have his affairs prepared and that a niece wanted to steal all his money. Mrs. X. requested that the attorney see Mr. C. at the hospital and draw up a will. Mr. C. told him he wished to bequeath three-fourths of his estate to his sister, one fourth to his niece and because he was afraid Mr. and Mrs. X. would put him out in the street if they found out he left nothing to them, decided to leave $2,000 to Mrs. X. Mr. C. denied any knowledge of a recently opened savings account he had opened in trust for Mrs. X. and wanted it changed back into his name alone. The attorney drew up the will pursuant to Mr. C.'s instructions, requested the hospital refrain from putting Mr. C. under sedation so he could sign with a clear mind. Mrs. X. learned Mr. C. had made provisions for his own family and had made a specific bequest for the X.'s. When the attorney returned to the hospital with the proposed will and a letter directing the name change on the account, he was barred entrance to Mr. C.'s room by personnel who claimed Mr. C. was under heavy sedation and was asked to leave. Mr. C. died 2 days later while under the care of the doctor who serviced the residents of the adult home. A Surrogate Court eventually returned the money to Mr. C.'s estate.

- New York supplied numerous other cases of abuse which took place in boarding homes, also known as adult care homes in New York. In one instance, the boarding home operator withdrew some $22,000 in checks payable to a senior citizen and had them endorsed over to him. When confronted, the operator protested that the money had been used to take the woman and his wife on a brief trip to Florida. The woman died without recovering her money. Another woman claimed that some $3,000 in silver and personal items was taken by the operator of another home. Authorities discovered this theft and the operator restored about half of the items to her. She said she tolerated the practice because the operator said he would tell the authorities she was crazy and no one would believe her. In a third case noted above, another boarding home owner took about $3,400 from a 79-year-old woman who suffered from chronic brain syndrome and confusion. He wrote a will leaving the woman's estate to himself and his wife. Following the woman's death from a pulmonary embolism, a Westchester Surrogate Court voided this will as a product of fraud and undue influence.

- A 76-year-old North Carolina woman, who could no longer manage her own affairs or care for herself refused to allow her daughter to sell her property (mother's). However, the daughter soon did so against her mother's will and would not turn over the proceeds from the sale of the property to her mother.

- Also in North Carolina, an elderly woman in ill health required hospitalization. Following her convalescence, family members would not allow her to return home. They placed her in a boarding home where she felt she did not need to be. She learned that a guardian had been appointed to manage her affairs and that checks were being written on her behalf to pay for her care in the boarding home. She found herself unable to get access to her checking account or any of her funds. She did not have money enough to have her hair done or even to buy a soft drink. Her pleas to see an eye doctor, along with her plea to be allowed to return home where she could have some semblance of dignity and privacy, went unheeded.

- Pennsylvania reported a case where authorities have attempted to get an 89-year-old father to file charges against an alcoholic son who forces him to turn over his monthly social security check. When the father refuses, he is tied to a chair so he can't leave the house.

- A Pennsylvania attorney submitted the following case which involved an elderly man, "Mike," who was financially abused by his daughter, "Barbara." Mike was an ill-educated man who had been a teamster driver and dock loader until his retirement in 1972. He had twice served in the U.S. Army for a total of seven years. He and his wife, from whom he separated in 1953, had 3 children of whom Barbara was the oldest. She was in her mid-forties when problems began.

On March 2, 1975, as Mike was driving home from a party, he was hit broadside by an uninsured motorist and suffered three fractured ribs, ankle fracture and a fracture and dislocation of his left hip. Particularly because of the broken hip, he went through an extensive hospital course. After the hip was set in the hospital, Mike was transferred to a nursing home. While there, the hip was dislocated and he was readmitted to the hospital for a total hip replacement. His daughter was dissatisfied with treatment there and had him transferred to another hospital where the hip dislocated again and corrective surgery was performed. He was then discharged to a nursing home for further recuperation, then returned to the hospital for final evaluation, then discharged. A week later, another hip dislocation necessitated an operation to replace an artificial component of the hip joint. After his release, dislocation again recurred, but relocation of the hip was successful and no additional dislocation occurred. His treatment period extended from March 3, 1975 through October 18, 1975.

During hospitalization periods, Mike was receiving his teamster pension, social security, and uninsured motorist benefits, all of which he instructed his daughter Barbara to put in his bank account, with her name on his checking account to pay his bills. She was given permission to keep his teamster pension checks for her "trouble." Hospitalization insurance policies paid him benefits for days in hospitals or nursing homes. After final discharge, Mike moved into Barbara's home. He was bedfast for a

3-month period, but by June of 1976, was able to walk with the help of a cane and eventually made a full recovery.

During his hospitalization, Mike was asked by Barbara's husband to pay off a $5,500 mortgage on their home. This was deducted from his bank account for "services." In March 1976, Mike wanted to buy a car and learned his bank account had $3,000 less than it should have. He moved to his brother's home and Barbara petitioned the court to be made guardian of his person and his estate on the grounds he was incompetent. Her requested emergency hearing was dismissed.

Mike obtained the services of an attorney whose investigation revealed that Mike had received retirement and insurance benefits totalling more than $42,000, of which less than $6,000 could be accounted for. A suit for a total of $36,000 plus interest was filed against Barbara who had deposited most of her father's money in a joint bank account of her and her husband. Prior to the trial, Mike wanted to drop the case and when her attorney offered to settle the case for $10,000, Mike wanted to take the offer because he did not want to testify in court against his daughter. The day before the case was to be heard in court, Barbara's attorney made a final offer which Mike accepted.

From the amount of $36,000, the sum of $8,000 for documented expenses paid for Mike's benefit by Barbara was to be deducted; $5,000 was to be deducted as compensation for her services and his room and board. For the remaining $17,500, Mike was to have a mortgage to Barbara's house in the amount of $15,500 plus 6% interest and Barbara would give Mike $2,000 cash at the time of settlement execution. The mortgage has been paid timely in monthly installments to Mike, but Barbara, in her court deposition, berated her father for his ingratitude and proclaimed she deserved the entire amount of money. Ironically, she would have inherited his entire estate as per his will, which was redrawn after the financial abuse.

- In South Carolina, caseworkers found an 80-year-old woman who was bedfast and neglected by her son who tied her to the bed and locked the bedroom door, leaving her all alone during the day and much of the night. The son expropriated her social security check and other financial assets.

- Texas caseworkers reported that a 102-year-old woman who was almost blind, lived independently in her own home along with an adopted son and granddaughter. One of the elderly woman's other granddaughters moved into the home along with her teenage children who proceeded to demolish the home and to steal their great grandmother's money. The old woman and her adopted son and granddaughter asked the newcomers to leave. They refused. As a result of the conflict, the elderly woman was thrown out of her own home into the street.

- In Washington, a grandson refused to provide medical attention for his dependent grandmother who suffered from terminal cancer. He stated he did not want the woman's income and property needlessly depleted.

141

In addition to being abused physically and financially, the elderly can also suffer emotional or psychological abuse at the hands of their relatives. At one end of the spectrum, psychological abuse includes simple name calling and verbal assaults. At the other end, it is a protracted and systematic effort to dehumanize the elderly, sometimes with the goal of driving a person to insanity or suicide. There are few things more pernicious in life than the constant threat by caretakers to throw the elderly into the street or have them committed to mental institutions. The most common weapon used in this warfare is the threat of nursing home placement. This kind of activity is associated more with concentration camps than with private homes where the elderly reside. However, several examples of these almost unspeakable offenses have come to the attention of the Committee. By definition, psychological abuse usually exists in combination with one or more other abuses. Following are some examples:

- In Massachusetts, an immigrant woman in her 70's with visual problems and minor infirmities moved into her niece's home and shared expenses. The niece began to misappropriate her aunt's checks, locked up the food and starved her. On one occasion, she started deportation proceedings against her aunt and constantly threatened her with nursing home placement.

- In Massachusetts, a daughter-in-law harbored great resentment of her mother-in-law for whose care she was responsible. The daughter-in-law refused to contribute to the woman's support. The daughter-in-law converted her mother-in-law's social security checks to her own use—often to buy alcohol. Over a long period of time, the elderly woman was verbally abused, threatened, and in fact, the daughter-in-law did periodically beat the woman. When this matter came to the attention of the police, they discovered that the daughter-in-law put the woman's food on the floor, telling her she was an animal and that she would be required to eat like one.

- A report from Delaware tells of a daughter-in-law who would keep her husband's widowed mother confined in the basement without social contacts. Any time the widow tried to leave this captivity, she was verbally assaulted. After the widow broke her arm in a fall, the daughter-in-law added physical force, severely twisting the woman's broken arm on several occasions.

- An 87-year-old woman in Massachusetts was psychologically abused by her middle-aged son. On a visit to her on a day when she was not feeling well, he proceeded to discuss what monies she had, what insurance, and what brothers or sisters of his were to get her property in the event of her death. The conversation disturbed her greatly and the day after the discussion she went to bed, and never got out of it. One month later, she was dead.

- In California, an 87-year-old woman in ill-health, confined to a wheelchair, and unable to care for her daily needs, was repeatedly and systematically abused by her family and nurse-companion. The mental and physical torture lasted six years. During this time, the woman was threatened, held prisoner, deprived of all contact with the outside world, not permitted to see friends

142

and family, and battered. Her nurse-companion (conservator)
and three children with the knowledge of the victim's bank and
attorney, depleted her assets by $292,000 as well as 200 shares of
Caterpillar Tractor stock.

- In New Jersey, a young man threatened his grandmother for
months in order to extort money with which to buy drugs. The
boy's mother (the victim's daughter) was also a drug addict.

- In a mid-Western State, an 85-year-old woman was allowed to
lay covered with urine and feces for so long that bedsores developed which became infested with maggots. The granddaughter, apparently oblivious of her responsibility toward the old
woman, frequently abandoned her charge, in one instance flying
to Hawaii with a friend. The weapon with which the granddaughter enforced her will, was the threat of nursing home placement. The old woman was terrified at the prospect.

- Social workers in West Virginia recently received a telephone
call telling them that a 92-year-old woman was being confined
in a trailer behind her children's home against her will. Upon
investigation, the daughter and son-in-law admitted that they
had locked the woman in the trailer when "she got out of hand—
she just wants to go out all the time, you can't do anything with
her," said the daughter. When the workers suggested that the
woman could be cared for in a day care center, they were rebuffed
by the family who refused them further access to the victim.
At last report, the woman had fallen, broken her arm, and had
been hospitalized.

- In a Delaware case, an elderly woman reported she had been
repeatedly threatened by her son. The threats were verbal at first
but later the son purchased a gun and used it to terrorize his
mother. Several violent episodes had taken place before the in-
valid woman, who suffered from an amputated foot, signed a
warrant for her son's arrest. The woman did not show up in
Court for the hearing which was scheduled. The reason she did
not do so is unclear. The reason offered was that her physical
condition did not allow her to make the appearance.

- In Michigan, a 79-year-old man was reportedly threatened by his
28-year-old son. The son was alleged to have a drug dependency
problem and converted his father's social security checks to supply his habit. The father admitted he was intimidated by and
lived in fear of his son. Social services workers helped the reluctant father initiate eviction proceedings against the son. Dur-
this process the father had to be relocated temporarily in other
living accommodations for his own protection.

- An elderly woman living in the District of Columbia was confined to the cellar by her daughter-in-law who verbally abused
her on a daily basis. Predictably, there were outbursts of physical abuse to enforce this confinement.

- Another elderly woman in the District of Columbia was recently
found to have been held a virtual prisoner against her will. This
time the abuser was her husband who was caring for her.

- In the District of Columbia, caseworkers found a severely under-
fed 86-year-old man lying in a filthy, roach-infested apartment.
The man told them that his son had threatened to shoot him if

he let anyone in the house. He said he was fed noodles with maggots in them and that his son had threatened to put embalming fluid in his food.

VIOLATION OF RIGHTS

All Americans, whether young or old, rich or poor, well or sick, are invested with certain inalienable rights by the United States Constitution. In addition, further rights are conferred by Federal statutes and the interpretation of them (and the Constitution) by Federal Courts. In addition, there are other rights which have been granted to citizens by the respective States through their legislatures and preserved through their courts.

This section of this report sets forth only a few of those enumerated rights along with examples of how these rights have been breached or vitiated by family members who are placed in the position of providing care and assistance to their elders.

1. The right to personal liberty.—The right to move freely, the right not to be imprisoned in one's home, the right to be free from physical restraints, are at the very essence of American democracy. However, there have been numerous examples in the preceding pages of older Americans being held captive against their will, virtual prisoners in their own homes. There have also been numerous cases of individuals who have been restrained with ropes and wire, tied to their bed as well as locked in their rooms or homes:

> . . . A 19-year-old Illinois woman confessed to torturing her 81-year-old father and chaining him to a toilet for 7 days. She also hit him with a hammer when he was asleep. After she made him weak enough, she chained his legs together. . . .

2. The right to adequate appropriate medical treatment.—The right to prompt quality medical care and the right to some participation in medical decisions are no less basic to Americans. The preceding pages, however, provide numerous examples where the elderly have been deprived of medical care by relatives who did not want to deplete the senior's assets, spend money of their own or lose the use of the senior's income. The case histories throughout this section confirm the hypothesis that a great number of America's seniors are not receiving the medical care they need. For example:

> . . . In Washington, an 84-year-old woman terminally ill with cancer was refused proper medical attention by her grandson who did not want the woman's property and income dissipated by doctor and hospital payments. The woman was found in tremendous pain living in truly wretched conditions. The victim was transferred to a nursing home where she died a few weeks later. . . .

3. The right not to have one's property taken without due process of law.—The preceding pages are replete with examples of relatives who have taken the property of the elderly and converted it to their own use. Sometimes this has been accomplished by force or through the use of weapons, in other instances, it has been accomplished by stealth through deceit and fraud. As the subsection on financial abuse indicates, the elderly are all too often easy victims of schemes to deprive them of their property. For example:

144

. . . New Jersey officials reported a case where title to a woman's home had been turned over to her son, an attorney, apparently without the woman's knowledge or permission. Caseworkers were unsuccessful in their efforts to restore title of the home because of the unavailability of legal assistance. . . .

4. The right to freedom of assembly, speech, and religion.—These protections specifically enumerated in the Bill of Rights have also been abridged and vitiated. Older Americans in many instances have been prevented from communicating with neighbors or friends. They have been prevented from having others in their home. In several instances, they have been denied access to the telephone and not allowed to receive mail unopened. In a number of cases reported heretofore, the elderly have been afraid to speak in front of their caretakers. No specific cases were received relating to breaching the right to practice religion, however, it is likely that this right has been abridged by some relatives of some senior citizens somewhere in America. The following is an example of an abrogation of this particular right:

. . . In California, an 87-year-old woman in ill-health, confined to a wheelchair and unable to care for her daily needs was repeatedly and systematically abused by her family and nurse companion. The mental and physical torture lasted six years. During this time, the woman was threatened, held prisoner, deprived of all contact with the outside world, not permitted to see friends and family, and battered. Her nurse-companion (conservator) and three children with the knowledge of the victim's bank and attorney, depleted her assets by $292,000 as well as 200 shares of Caterpillar Tractor stock.

5. The right to freedom from forced labor.—The United States Supreme Court has upheld this right and yet many older Americans, as can be seen from the following example, have been forced to work to support indolent sons and daughters who collect the paychecks received by many of the elderly.

. . . Caseworkers in Maryland told the Committee about a 67-year-old widow who was regularly beaten by her 35-year-old son. The widow was forced to turn all her property and assets over to the son who stopped working. When the income and money from property had been exhausted, the two subsisted on her $80 a month social security check. The widow did some babysitting to supplement this income.

6. The right to freedom from sexual abuse.—As noted from the preceding examples, some seniors are not free from sexual abuse by their relatives and in-laws. In some cases, such abuse is carried out by force, sometimes enforced through the use of weapons. For example:

. . . In the District of Columbia, an 80-year-old woman, a paraplegic, had been sexually abused over a 6-year period by her son-in-law, who beat her with a hammer when she refused his advances. . . .

7. The right to freedom from verbal abuse.—Many senior citizens are being verbally abused on a daily basis by their relatives. The seniors often feel that they have little choice but to put up with such abuse. They believe that they are powerless to stop it and should they try, it would mean that care or food would be denied to them or that they would be forced out into the street or into a nursing home. For example:

 . . . In Michigan, a 79-year-old man was reportedly threatened by his 28-year-old son. The son was alleged to have a drug dependency problem and converted his father's social security checks to supply his habit. The father admitted he was intimidated by and lived in fear of his son who showered the old man with profanity on a daily basis. Social service workers helped the reluctant father initiate eviction proceedings against the son. During this process, the father had to be relocated temporarily in other living accommodations for his own protection.

 8. The right to privacy.—The U.S. Constitution and related laws recognize a right of all citizens to a certain sphere of privacy. Unfortunately, as can be seen from the examples in the preceding pages, privacy is very often denied to the elderly by their relatives. Quite often the denial of privacy is used as a weapon in the psychological war against the elderly carried out by their caretakers. For example:

 . . . A woman in Missouri, age 77, who had suffered a recent stroke and was bedridden was left in the care of her only son who was in his early 40's and on welfare. The son was a diabetic and suffered from asthma. The two people lived in a rowhouse confining themselves to the top floor bedrooms, cooking on a hot plate, and washing dishes in the bathtub. Since the son had 20 to 30 cats, the house was extremely filthy and filled with cat feces. Although many agencies tried to intervene, the occupants would permit no one to visit or clean the house. The son was married about four or five years although he intimated that the marriage was never consummated. The daughter-in-law who had since remarried still visited her mother-in-law. The son owned two or three motorcycles and had an extensive gun collection plus a room full of World War II mementos. Occasionally, he worked as a drummer in a nightclub and was frequently known to become drunk and violent. He had often beaten his mother who would contact the police when he did so. The police, aware of the problem, were often able to calm the son. At other times, he threatened to kill her and stated he wished she were dead. Although she was frequently ill and required constant health care, and had virtually no privacy, health aides sent to the house were threatened by physical violence by the son and were afraid to return. . . .

 9. The right to a clean, safe living environment.—This right is another which is frequently breached with far-ranging consequences to the elderly. One result from the lack of clean living conditions can be illness, and another can be death. The following example is a violation of this right:

 . . . In South Carolina, a 68-year-old woman living with her daughter was found by a caseworker in conditions of unspeakable squalor. The woman was kept in an unheated portion of the house where the temperature was measured at less than 20 degrees. When found, the woman had eight soiled blankets piled over her head to keep her warm and the urine from her catheter was frozen. She was also found to be malnourished. She developed pneumonia and was hospitalized. Upon discharge, authorities had her placed in a nursing home.

10. The right not to be declared incompetent and committed to a mental institution without due process of law.—State laws which allow family members to commit their elderly relatives vary widely. In some States, it is a fairly easy matter to effect such commitment, in others it is more difficult. As noted, some elderly people are adjudged incompetent upon affidavits from family members who have their own motives, usually related to obtaining possession of the financial resources of the aged person. For example:

> A 74-year-old Florida woman claims to have been taken to a mental hospital in the middle of the night, committed without the examination of two doctors. Her daughter, and a psychiatrist she claims never examined or questioned her, signed commitment papers. Her home was then sold. She states her hospital papers diagnose her as having chronic brain syndrome and her attorney has termed her incompetent.

11. The right to complain and seek redress of grievances.—The case histories in this section show that oftentimes seniors are not allowed to complain or to seek redress of their grievances from other agencies. Attempts to do so have been met with threats of violence or with reprisals of all kinds, including further loss of rights and privileges. For example:

> . . . An anonymous caller reported to the Michigan Department of Human Services that a 65-year-old woman was being beaten by her children with whom she lived. On the first visit, the woman denied the beatings, since the children were in the home at the time. On subsequent visits, however, when the children were absent, she freely admitted to the beatings and wanted help.

12. The right to vote and exercise all the rights of citizens.—As can be seen from the cases in this section, these rights are not always protected. Senior Americans, under the domination of their younger relatives and caretakers, all too often find they are on the outside of the American participatory democracy. It is obvious from the aforementioned cases that the rights of the elderly are often abridged by their own relatives.

13. The right to be treated with courtesy, dignity, and respect.—It goes without saying from all the above that far too many elderly are not being protected in this basic right. For example:

> . . . In Massachusetts, a daughter-in-law harbored great resentment of her mother-in-law for whose care she was responsible. The daughter-in-law refused to contribute to the woman's support. The daughter-in-law converted her mother-in-law's social security check to her own use, often to buy alcohol. Over a long period of time, the elderly woman was verbally abused, threatened, and in fact, the daughter-in-law periodically beat the woman. When this matter came to the

attention of the police, they discovered that the daughter-in-law put the woman's food on the floor, telling her she was an animal and that she would be required to eat like one.

SELF NEGLECT

It should be no surprise to most people to learn that many older Americans neglect their personal needs or that they sometimes abuse themselves. Generally, neglect is a function of diminished physical or mental ability. Self abuse can sometimes be associated with senility or other forms of mental disability brought on by old age. Self abuse and self neglect are also brought on in some cases by external forces which cause a conscious or unconscious indifference to one's personal welfare and well being. In the extreme, such cases may end in suicide; it is no secret that suicide rates are very high among the aged in American society.

Within the context of this report, self-neglect is considered to the extent that such neglect is brought on or exacerbated by the actions of relatives and their attitudes towards their loved ones. Most of the cases received by the Committee involved older people living alone and abandoned by their families. In old age, the social distances between them and their friends and loved ones have grown wider. According to experts such as Dr. Robert Butler, Director of the National Institute on Aging, and Dr. Carl Eisendorfer of the University of Washington, loneliness, despair, and rejection by one's loved ones can often give rise to feelings of worthlessness and serve to snuff out the will to live.

A number of cases are provided below which illustrate this point. Several examples related to elderly people living with loved ones where one or both parties are physically or mentally incapable of providing the care, food, and attention that is necessary to sustain life.

- In Louisiana, a 90-year-old man was living in an isolated area abandoned by relatives. He was found with his legs covered with open ulcers. He had 20 to 25 dogs which he slept with to keep warm. Even though his windows were boarded up, a terrible odor permeated outdoors. He would allow no one entrance to his home. It was later discovered that he had not had a bath in over a year; he went only once a month to buy groceries; and the groceries he did buy with his meager income and food stamps was spent on food for the dogs. The older man was eventually convinced to temporarily relocate to a nursing home where it took three scrub-downs to clean the patient.

- Connecticut reported that an elderly woman was living alone in a decaying house which had a putrid odor. She was found to be obese with a grossly swollen, infected and ulcerated leg with deep lesions exposing the bone and pustules extending to her foot. A cousin who had been appointed her conservator three years before did little except pay her bills. Food was delivered, but there was no working refrigerator. Her bed was a filthy, stained, torn couch. Her floors and carpet were stained with blood and drainage from her foot. She denied the need for and refused medical help. The case was finally referred to protective services and the woman was taken to a hospital on probate court order to examine the need for leg amputation.

- An 80-year-old Nebraska woman, abandoned by her family, was

148

reported by a neighbor to be wandering about her yard and clinging to her fence for support—not appearing to know what she was doing. It was discovered by social workers that the woman had not seen a doctor since July 1977, but was having a prescription filled at several pharmacies. The prescription was to be filled once a month, but at one time it was filled six times in two months at one pharmacy and six times in two months at a second pharmacy. Her medication regimen has since been corrected after consultation with her doctor and family.

- An elderly New Jersey woman living in an apartment building for older persons was reported by a friend to have been wandering about in the building and out in the cold streets for a long time. The friend said the police regularly brought her back when they found her barefoot on the street. A month previously, she was found sitting on the top landing of the fourth floor of her building with her money spread all around her.

- Louisiana reported an elderly client with diabetes and an amputation living alone in a house with no screens. Neighbors would periodically feed the client and attempt to keep flies off the wounds. The client's son was out of town but refused to have the client placed in a nursing home where proper care could be given because he was fearful the nursing home would use the older client's life insurance for payment and the son wouldn't get it.

- The same State also reported an 85-year-old woman living in a burned house with no utilities. She was known in the community as a "beggar" and would not use her income for necessities. She would cook on an open fire in her yard. Social workers verified that the older woman had no income—she gave all her savings to her children who refused to care for her.

- Maine advised the Committee of an abandoned elderly woman who was threatened with eviction due to drinking excessively and causing disturbances. Workers found the older woman in a debilitating state from alcoholism. She would not allow anyone entrance into her apartment. Because she was not doing or threatening harm to others, admittance could not be forced. Two days later, she was found dead in her apartment.

- An 85-year-old Arizona woman, living alone, ignored by relatives, was referred to the Department of Human Services by a nurse who was contacted by an individual concerned about the older woman's well-being. A home visit found the house infested with fleas, roaches, ticks, black widows, cats, dogs, etc. The elderly woman had not had a change of clothing or a bath in several years. Her clothes were encrusted with food, urine and feces. Her toenails had grown so much that they were curled under. Further investigation indicated that the older woman was wealthy, but unable to take care of her own affairs. She was feeding the dogs, but not herself. In-home care and services were finally provided.

- In the District of Columbia, a 90-year-old woman, confused and hallucinating, was moved from her home to a general hospital as a social emergency. She had been found in a basement apartment, without food or care, and with the body of her son who had died three days prior. Neighborhood youths were robbing her at will.

● The following case history was supplied to the Committee by a social worker in Texas. Her summarized story is as follows:

I made a visit to a mobile home (8' x 40') which was totally closed in with absolutely no windows open. Even outdoors there was a strong odor of various types of waste. I knocked at the door and introduced myself. An elderly man hesitantly opened the door (merely a crack) and asked what I wanted. I explained that we had received a report about his elderly wife and we wanted to help. At that time, he opened the door ajar and asked that I find myself a way into the house through all the rubbish. As he opened the door, I observed him as being an extremely obese individual, about 70-years of age, who was wearing clothing on his body which actually shined from the accumulation of grease and grime. His clothes also appeared to be stained with feces and urine. As I poked my head through the door, I noticed a thin, frail old lady sitting in a corner on the couch. She was totally nude from the waist up and was wearing filthy jeans which appeared to be twenty sizes too big for her. They were obviously the older man's jeans. She was totally confused and abusively demanded that I go away. She kept complaining of a sharp, stabbing pain in her back and kept insisting that the older man rub her back. She was sitting on the living room couch in her own waste (for several days) and had feces underneath her long fingernails and on her shoes and feet. Her hair, which appeared to be an original grey, was matted together with natural oils as well as food and possibly feces. There were two pots underneath the dining table full of urine and pieces of clothing scattered everywhere which appeared to have been used as diapers (for bowel movements) several days or weeks before. The home was definitely in a state of shambles. The trash, clothing, etc. prohibited anyone from gaining entrance. The floor which was an original gold carpet was completely full of small pebble-like particles. Later, the older man revealed that he would pour cat litter on the spilled urine. He was using the cat litter as a disinfectant. The elderly woman was eventually hospitalized and it was determined that she had a broken 5th vertebrae. Later, both were placed in a nursing home.

SUMMARY

It should be clear from the hundreds of examples in this chapter that abuse of the elderly by their loved ones and caretakers is a widespread problem. The Committee received examples from every State. Only a few of these are reprinted here. The examples are illustrative and typical; they are not the most horrible cases that can be found. The examples of physical, sexual, financial and psychological abuse of the elderly by their loved ones are truly repugnant. It is hard to accept the fact that these listed abuses are not isolated incidents but part of a continuing pattern of abuse perpetrated by sons and daughters against their parents. Since it is clear that elder abuse is a major American problem which has yet to be recognized, it remains for other chapters to provide additional documentation of the size of the problem, to develop what the states are doing about it and to suggest what to do about it.

INDEX